Everyday
plant based

Publications International, Ltd.

Pictured on the front cover: Asian Tofu Salad *(page 40)*.

Pictured on the back cover *(clockwise from top left):* Crustless Spinach Quiche *(page 5),* Portobello Provolone Panini *(page 130),* Roasted Brussels Sprouts Salad *(page 26),* Linguine with Sun-Dried Tomato Pesto *(page 26),* Quinoa and Mango Salad *(page 69)* and Cabbage Colcannon *(page 152).*

Photograph on front cover and page 41 copyright © Shutterstock.com.

ISBN: 978-1-64558-602-9

Manufactured in China.

8 7 6 5 4 3 2 1

Let's get social!
 @Publications_International
@PublicationsInternational
www.pilbooks.com

contents

breakfast

Crustless Spinach Quiche

Makes 6 servings

8 eggs

1 cup half-and-half

1 teaspoon Italian seasoning

¾ teaspoon salt

½ teaspoon black pepper

1 package (10 ounces) frozen chopped spinach, thawed and squeezed dry

1¼ cups (5 ounces) shredded Italian cheese blend

1. Preheat oven to 350°F. Spray 8-inch round baking pan with nonstick cooking spray.

2. Beat eggs, half-and-half, Italian seasoning, salt and pepper in medium bowl until well blended. Stir in spinach and cheese; mix well. Pour into prepared pan.

3. Bake 33 minutes or until toothpick inserted into center comes out clean. Remove to wire rack; cool 10 minutes before serving.

4. To remove quiche from pan, run knife around edge of pan to loosen. Invert quiche onto plate; invert again onto second plate. Cut into wedges to serve.

Almond French Toast with Peach Compote

Makes 4 servings

Peach Compote

- 3 **tablespoons sugar**
- ½ **cup water**
- 1½ **cups fresh sliced peeled peaches or thawed frozen sliced peaches, drained**
- 2 **tablespoons peach fruit spread**
- ¼ **teaspoon ground cinnamon**

French Toast

- ¼ **cup plain almond milk or regular milk**
- 3 **tablespoons sugar**
- 2 **eggs**
- 2 **egg whites**
- ½ **teaspoon almond extract**
- ⅛ **teaspoon salt**
- 4 **slices multigrain bread**
- ⅓ **cup sliced almonds**
- 2 **teaspoons vegetable oil**

1. For compote, combine 3 tablespoons sugar and ½ cup water in medium saucepan; cook and stir over medium heat until dissolved. Add peaches; bring to a boil over medium-high heat. Reduce heat to medium; cook 5 minutes or until peaches soften. Stir in fruit spread; cook 1 minute or until thickened. Remove from heat; stir in cinnamon. Cover and keep warm.

2. For French toast, whisk almond milk and 3 tablespoons sugar in large shallow dish until sugar dissolves. Whisk in eggs, egg whites, almond extract and salt. Place bread in dish; let stand about 3 minutes or until egg mixture is absorbed, turning once. Sprinkle both sides of bread slices evenly with almonds, pressing to adhere.

3. Brush large nonstick skillet with oil; heat over medium-high heat. Add bread; cook 2 to 3 minutes per side or until lightly browned. Serve toast topped with compote.

Roasted Tomato Quiche

Makes 6 servings

- 1 pint grape tomatoes
- 1 tablespoon olive oil
  Salt and black pepper
- 2½ cups riced cauliflower (fresh or frozen)
- ½ cup Parmesan cheese
- 6 eggs, divided
- ¾ teaspoon salt, divided
- ½ teaspoon black pepper, divided
- ¾ cup milk
- ½ cup (2 ounces) shredded mozzarella cheese
- 2 cloves garlic, minced
- ½ teaspoon fresh thyme leaves

1. Preheat oven to 350°F. Place tomatoes in shallow baking dish; drizzle with oil and sprinkle lightly with salt and pepper. Bake 1 hour, stirring once or twice.

2. Spray 9-inch pie plate with nonstick cooking spray. Place cauliflower in large microwavable bowl; cover with plastic wrap and cut slit to vent. Microwave on HIGH 4 minutes; stir. Cover and cook on HIGH 4 minutes. Remove cover; cool slightly. Place cauliflower on double layer of paper towels; fold over paper towels and squeeze to remove excess moisture. Return to bowl. Add Parmesan cheese, 1 egg, ½ teaspoon salt and ¼ teaspoon pepper; mix well. Press onto bottom and up side of prepared pie plate. *Increase oven temperature to 425°F.* Bake crust 15 minutes. Remove from oven; place on sheet pan.

3. *Reduce oven temperature to 375°F.* Whisk 5 eggs, milk, mozzarella cheese, garlic, thyme, remaining ¼ teaspoon salt and remaining ¼ teaspoon black pepper in medium bowl until well blended. Place tomatoes in crust; pour egg mixture over tomatoes. Bake 45 minutes or until thin knife inserted into center comes out clean (a little cheese is okay). Cool 10 minutes before slicing.

Note: To make riced cauliflower, cut 1 head of cauliflower into 1-inch florets. Working in batches, pulse the florets until they form small rice-size pieces. If there are any large chunks left behind, pick them out and add them to your next batch. Or grate a whole head of cauliflower on the large holes of a box grater into a large bowl, rotating until all the florets are shredded.

Spiced Pumpkin Muffins

Makes 12 muffins

½ cup slivered almonds

2 cups all-purpose flour

2 teaspoons baking powder

1 teaspoon baking soda

1 teaspoon salt

½ teaspoon ground cinnamon

½ teaspoon ground nutmeg

¼ teaspoon ground ginger

¼ teaspoon ground cloves

1 cup packed brown sugar

¾ cup canned pumpkin

2 eggs

½ cup vegetable or canola oil

1 cup powdered sugar

2 to 3 tablespoons orange or lemon juice

1. Preheat oven to 350°F. Spray 12 standard (2½-inch) muffin cups with nonstick cooking spray or line with paper baking cups. Spread almonds in small baking pan. Bake 5 to 7 minutes or until golden brown, stirring occasionally. Immediately remove from pan; cool completely.

2. Combine flour, baking powder, baking soda, salt, cinnamon, nutmeg, ginger and cloves in medium bowl; mix well. Combine brown sugar, pumpkin, eggs and oil in large bowl; beat until well blended. Add flour mixture; stir just until dry ingredients are moistened. Stir in almonds. Spoon batter evenly into prepared muffin cups.

3. Bake 20 to 22 minutes or until toothpick inserted into centers comes out clean. Cool in pan 5 minutes; remove to wire rack to cool completely.

4. Place powdered sugar in small bowl. Add 2 tablespoons orange juice; whisk until smooth. Add additional juice if necessary to reach drizzling consistency. Drizzle glaze over muffins; let stand until set.

Chorizo Hash

Makes 4 servings

2 unpeeled russet potatoes, cut into ½-inch pieces

3 teaspoons salt, divided

6 to 8 ounces soy chorizo

1 yellow onion, chopped

½ red bell pepper, chopped (about ½ cup)

Fried, poached or scrambled eggs (optional)

Avocado slices (optional)

Fresh cilantro leaves (optional)

1. Fill medium saucepan half full with water. Add potatoes and 2 teaspoons salt; bring to a boil over high heat. Reduce heat to medium-low; cook about 8 minutes. (Potatoes will be firm.) Drain.

2. Meanwhile, heat large cast iron skillet over medium-high heat. Squeeze soy chorizo from plastic casing into skillet; cook and stir 5 minutes or until heated through, breaking into crumbles with wooden spoon. Add onion and bell pepper; cook and stir 4 minutes or until vegetables are softened.

3. Stir in potatoes and remaining 1 teaspoon salt; cook 10 to 15 minutes or until vegetables are tender and potatoes are lightly browned, stirring occasionally. Serve with eggs, if desired; garnish with avocado and cilantro.

Spinach Berry Smoothie

Makes 1 (10-ounce) serving

1½ cups ice cubes
½ banana
½ cup fresh raspberries
½ cup sliced fresh strawberries
½ cup fresh blueberries
½ cup packed torn spinach

1. Combine ice, banana, raspberries, strawberries, blueberries and spinach in blender; blend until smooth.

2. Pour into glass. Serve immediately.

Note: Fresh or frozen berries can be used to make this recipe. When using frozen fruit, reduce the amount of ice used.

Peaches & Cream Smoothie

Makes 3 (1-cup) servings

1 package (16 ounces) frozen peaches, partially thawed
2 containers (6 ounces each) vanilla or plain yogurt
¾ cup white grape juice or orange juice
2 tablespoons sugar or honey
½ teaspoon vanilla

1. Combine peaches, yogurt, grape juice, sugar and vanilla in blender; blend until smooth.

2. Pour into three glasses.

Vanilla Multigrain Waffles

Makes 4 waffles

1 cup buttermilk

¼ cup steel-cut oats

⅓ cup all-purpose flour

⅓ cup whole wheat flour

1 teaspoon baking powder

½ teaspoon baking soda

¼ teaspoon salt

1 egg

2 tablespoons packed brown sugar

1 tablespoon vegetable oil

1 teaspoon vanilla

Maple syrup (optional)

1. Combine buttermilk and oats in large bowl; let stand 10 minutes. Spray waffle maker with nonstick cooking spray; preheat according to manufacturer's directions.

2. Combine all-purpose flour, whole wheat flour, baking powder, baking soda and salt in medium bowl; mix well.

3. Whisk egg, brown sugar, oil and vanilla in small bowl until smooth and well blended. Stir into oat mixture. Add flour mixture; stir until smooth and well blended.

4. Pour ⅔ cup batter into waffle maker; cook about 5 minutes or until steam stops escaping from around edges and waffle is golden brown. Repeat with remaining batter. Serve with maple syrup, if desired.

Garden Vegetable Muffins

Makes 12 muffins

  2 cups all-purpose flour
  2 tablespoons sugar
  1 tablespoon baking powder
  ¼ teaspoon salt
  3 ounces cream cheese
  ¾ cup milk
  ½ cup finely shredded or grated
      carrots
  ¼ cup chopped green onions
  ¼ cup vegetable oil
  1 egg

1. Preheat oven to 400°F. Spray 12 standard (2½-inch) muffin cups with nonstick cooking spray or line with paper baking cups.

2. Combine flour, sugar, baking powder and salt in large bowl. Cut in cream cheese with pastry blender or two knives until mixture resembles coarse crumbs.

3. Combine milk, carrots, green onions, oil and egg in small bowl until blended. Stir into flour mixture just until moistened. Spoon evenly into prepared muffin cups.

4. Bake 20 to 25 minutes or until toothpick inserted into centers comes out clean. Immediately remove from pan. Cool on wire rack 10 minutes. Serve warm.

Berry-Quinoa Parfaits

Makes 6 servings

⅔ cup uncooked quinoa

2 cups plus 2 tablespoons oatmilk or regular milk, divided

⅛ teaspoon salt

¼ cup sugar

1 egg

1½ teaspoons vanilla

2 cups sliced fresh strawberries

¼ cup vanilla yogurt (optional)

Ground cinnamon (optional)

1. Place quinoa in fine-mesh strainer; rinse well under cold water.

2. Combine quinoa, 2 cups oatmilk and salt in medium saucepan. Bring to a simmer over medium heat. Reduce heat to medium-low; simmer, uncovered, 10 to 15 minutes or until quinoa is tender, stirring frequently.

3. Whisk remaining 2 tablespoons milk, sugar, egg and vanilla in medium bowl until well blended. Gradually whisk ½ cup hot quinoa mixture into egg mixture, then whisk mixture back into saucepan. Cook over medium heat 3 to 5 minutes or until bubbly and thickened, stirring constantly. Remove from heat; let cool 30 minutes.

4. Layer quinoa mixture and strawberries in bowls. Top with yogurt and sprinkle with cinnamon, if desired.

Oatmeal with Berry Compote

Makes 4 servings

- 4 cups plus 1 tablespoon water, divided
- ½ teaspoon salt
- 1 cup steel-cut oats
- ½ teaspoon ground cinnamon
- ⅓ cup half-and-half or oatmilk
- ¼ cup packed brown sugar
- 1 cup fresh strawberries, hulled and quartered
- 1 container (6 ounces) fresh blackberries
- 1 container (6 ounces) fresh blueberries
- 3 tablespoons granulated sugar

1. Bring 4 cups water and salt to a boil in medium saucepan over medium-high heat. Whisk in oats and cinnamon. Reduce heat to medium; simmer, uncovered, 30 to 40 minutes or until water is absorbed and oats are tender. Remove from heat; stir in half-and-half and brown sugar.

2. Meanwhile, combine strawberries, blackberries, blueberries, granulated sugar and remaining 1 tablespoon water in small saucepan; bring to a simmer over medium heat. Cook 8 to 9 minutes or until berries are tender but still hold their shape, stirring occasionally.

3. Divide oatmeal among four bowls; top with berry compote.

salads

Heirloom Tomato Salad

Makes 4 servings

4 large lettuce leaves (Bibb, red or romaine)

2 large ripe heirloom tomatoes, sliced

1 cup grape or cherry tomatoes (yellow, red or a combination), halved

1 tablespoon olive oil

1 tablespoon balsamic glaze*

1 small clove garlic, minced

2 tablespoons thinly sliced fresh basil or chopped chives

2 tablespoons pine nuts, toasted**

Salt and black pepper

Look for balsamic glaze in the condiment or Italian section of the supermarket.

**To toast pine nuts, cook in small skillet over medium heat 1 to 2 minutes or until lightly browned, stirring frequently.*

1. Arrange lettuce leaves on four serving plates. Arrange tomatoes on lettuce.

2. Whisk oil, balsamic glaze and garlic in small bowl until emulsified and thick; drizzle over salad. Top with basil and pine nuts; season with salt and pepper.

Roasted Brussels Sprouts Salad

Makes 6 servings (about 8 cups)

Brussels Sprouts

- 1 **pound brussels sprouts, trimmed and halved**
- 2 **tablespoons olive oil**
- ½ **teaspoon salt**

Salad

- 2 **cups coarsely chopped baby kale**
- 2 **cups coarsely chopped romaine lettuce**
- 1½ **cups candied pecans**
- 1 **cup halved red grapes**
- 1 **cup diced cucumbers**
- ½ **cup fresh blueberries**
- ½ **cup chopped red onion**
- ½ **cup dried cranberries**
- ¼ **cup toasted pumpkin seeds (pepitas)**
- 1 **container (4 ounces) crumbled goat cheese**

Dressing

- ½ **cup olive oil**
- 6 **tablespoons balsamic vinegar**
- 6 **tablespoons strawberry jam**
- 2 **teaspoons Dijon mustard**
- 1 **teaspoon salt**

1. For brussels sprouts, preheat oven to 400°F. Spray large baking sheet with nonstick cooking spray.

2. Combine brussels sprouts, 2 tablespoons oil and ½ teaspoon salt in medium bowl; toss to coat. Arrange brussels sprouts in single layer on prepared baking sheet, cut sides down. Roast 20 minutes or until tender and browned, stirring once halfway through roasting. Cool completely on baking sheet.

3. For salad, combine kale, lettuce, pecans, grapes, cucumbers, blueberries, onion, cranberries and pumpkin seeds in large bowl. Top with brussels sprouts and cheese.

4. For dressing, whisk ½ cup oil, vinegar, jam, mustard and 1 teaspoon salt in small bowl until well blended. Pour over salad; toss gently to blend.

Veggie Pasta Salad

Makes 8 servings

8 ounces uncooked rotini pasta

2 cups carrot slices

4 cups broccoli florets

1½ cups chopped tomatoes

½ cup chopped green onions

1 cup mayonnalse (regular or vegan)

2 tablespoons white wine vinegar

1 tablespoon olive oil

1 tablespoon minced fresh basil *or* 1 teaspoon dried basil

2 teaspoons minced fresh oregano *or* ½ teaspoon dried oregano

1 clove garlic, minced

1 teaspoon sugar

1 teaspoon dry mustard

¼ teaspoon salt

¼ teaspoon black pepper

¼ cup grated Romano cheese (optional)

1. Bring large saucepan of salted water to a boil. Add pasta; cook 4 minutes. Add carrots; cook 1 minute. Add broccoli; cook 3 minutes or until vegetables are crisp-tender and pasta is tender. Immediately drain and run under cold water. Place in large bowl; add tomatoes and green onions.

2. Combine mayonnaise, vinegar, oil, basil, oregano, garlic, sugar, mustard, salt and pepper in medium bowl; mix well. Stir into pasta mixture. Add cheese, if desired; mix well. Refrigerate 3 hours or overnight to allow flavors to blend.

Tip: Check the cook time on your box of pasta to make sure it cooks to tender in 8 minutes. If it cooks in a different time or if you like your pasta more or less done, just add the carrots during the last 4 minutes of cooking and the broccoli during the last 3 minutes.

Tarragon Potato Salad

Makes 6 to 8 servings

6 medium red potatoes (about 1¾ pounds), scrubbed

2½ teaspoons salt, divided

1 cup frozen peas, thawed

¾ cup chopped green bell pepper

¾ cup mayonnaise (regular or vegan)

¼ cup milk or plain rice milk

¼ cup sliced green onions

2 tablespoons chopped fresh parsley

1 tablespoon lemon juice

2 teaspoons dried tarragon

¼ teaspoon black pepper

1. Place potatoes in medium saucepan; add water to cover and 2 teaspoons salt. Bring to a boil over medium-high heat; boil 25 minutes or until tender. Drain potatoes and let cool. Cut into slices when cool enough to handle.

2. Combine potatoes, peas and bell pepper in large bowl. Stir mayonnaise, milk, green onions, parsley, lemon juice, tarragon, remaining ½ teaspoon salt and black pepper in small bowl until smooth and well blended. Pour over potato mixture; gently toss to coat. Cover and refrigerate at least 4 hours before serving.

Spinach-Orange Salad with Lime Vinaigrette

Makes 6 servings

3 tablespoons lime juice

2 tablespoons vegetable oil

2 tablespoons sour cream

2¼ teaspoons sugar

¼ teaspoon salt

⅛ teaspoon red pepper flakes

Dash white pepper

1 large bunch spinach, stemmed *or* 1 package (5 ounces) baby spinach

2 oranges

½ small jicama, peeled and cut into julienne strips (about 1 cup)

¼ cup pecan halves, toasted*

*To toast pecans, spread in single layer in small heavy skillet. Cook over medium heat 1 to 2 minutes or until lightly browned, stirring frequently. Remove from skillet; cool before using.

1. For dressing, whisk lime juice, oil, sour cream, sugar, salt, red pepper flakes and white pepper in medium bowl until well blended.

2. Tear spinach into bite-size pieces; place in large bowl. Peel oranges, removing white membrane. Cut segments between membranes to remove; chop. Add oranges, jicama and pecans to spinach. Pour dressing over salad; toss gently until well mixed.

Springtime Panzanella

Makes 4 servings

3 tablespoons olive oil, divided

2 cloves garlic, minced and divided

3 slices whole wheat bread, cut into 1-inch cubes

1 teaspoon salt, divided

1 pound asparagus, cut into 1-inch pieces

¼ cup chopped carrot

½ cup finely chopped red onion

2 tablespoons white wine vinegar

1 tablespoon lemon juice

½ teaspoon Dijon mustard

2 tablespoons shredded Parmesan cheese (optional)

1. Preheat oven to 425°F. Spray two baking sheets with nonstick cooking spray.

2. Combine 1 tablespoon oil and 1 clove garlic in large bowl. Add bread cubes; toss to coat. Spread in single layer on one baking sheet. Combine 1 tablespoon oil, remaining 1 clove garlic and ½ teaspoon salt in same bowl. Add asparagus and carrot; toss to coat. Spread on second baking sheet.

3. Bake bread cubes and vegetables 15 minutes, stirring once. Let stand 5 to 10 minutes to cool slightly.

4. Meanwhile, combine onion, vinegar, remaining 1 tablespoon oil, lemon juice, mustard and remaining ½ teaspoon salt in same large bowl; mix well. Add bread cubes and vegetables; toss gently to coat. Top with cheese just before serving, if desired.

Coleslaw with Snow Peas and Corn

Makes 4 servings

- 4 cups (about 8 ounces) coleslaw mix
- ½ cup trimmed and thinly sliced snow peas
- ½ cup fresh or thawed frozen corn
- ¼ cup mayonnaise
- ¼ cup sour cream
- ¼ cup buttermilk
- 1 tablespoon cider vinegar
- 2 teaspoons sugar
- ¼ teaspoon celery seed

1. Combine coleslaw, snow peas and corn in large bowl.

2. Meanwhile, whisk mayonnaise, sour cream, buttermilk, vinegar, sugar and celery seed in medium bowl. Add to coleslaw mixture and mix to combine.

Sweet Potato and Corn Salad

Makes 4 to 6 servings

2 medium or 1 large sweet potato (about 12 ounces)

½ cup chopped green onions

½ cup chopped red bell pepper

½ cup fresh or thawed frozen corn

¼ cup salted peanuts

2 tablespoons olive oil

1 tablespoon lime juice

Pinch ground red pepper

Salt and black pepper

1. Pierce sweet potatoes in several places with fork and place in microwavable dish. Cover loosely with plastic wrap. Microwave on HIGH 6 to 7 minutes, turning over halfway through cooking. Let stand 10 minutes.

2. Peel sweet potatoes; cut into 1-inch pieces. Transfer to large bowl. Add green onions, bell pepper, corn and peanuts; mix well.

3. Whisk oil, lime juice and ground red pepper in small bowl. Season with salt and black pepper. Pour over sweet potato mixture; toss to coat. Serve immediately or refrigerate until ready to serve.

Asian Tofu Salad

Makes 4 to 6 servings

8 ounces firm tofu, drained

¼ cup rice vinegar

3 tablespoons soy sauce

1½ tablespoons sugar

1 tablespoon toasted sesame oil

1 to 2 teaspoons chili garlic sauce

1 teaspoon grated fresh ginger

1 tablespoon vegetable oil

8 cups mixed salad greens

1 cup quartered grape tomatoes

½ cup thinly sliced red onion or shallots

1 cup thinly sliced cucumber (optional)

1 carrot, shredded (optional)

¼ cup coarsely chopped walnuts or dry-roasted peanuts

1. Cut tofu into ½-inch cubes, place in single layer on paper towels to drain. Pat dry.

2. Combine rice vinegar, soy sauce, sugar, sesame oil, chili garlic sauce and ginger in small bowl.

3. Heat vegetable oil in large nonstick skillet over medium-high heat. Add tofu; cook 5 minutes or until tofu is lightly browned, turning occasionally. Add 2 tablespoons sauce mixture; cook and stir 1 minute or until tofu is glazed. Let cool slightly.

4. Place greens in large bowl; add tomatoes, onion, cucumber and carrot, if desired. Drizzle with remaining sauce mixture and toss to mix. Divide salad among salad bowls; top with tofu and walnuts.

Veggie and White Bean Salad

Makes 4 servings

1 can (about 15 ounces) navy beans, rinsed and drained

1 can (14 ounces) quartered artichoke hearts, drained

1 green bell pepper, chopped

1 yellow bell pepper, chopped

1 cup grape tomatoes, halved

¼ cup chopped fresh basil or parsley

¼ cup olive oil

3 tablespoons red wine vinegar

1 clove garlic, minced

1 teaspoon Dijon mustard

½ teaspoon black pepper

¼ teaspoon salt

1 package (4 ounces) crumbled feta cheese with sun-dried tomatoes and basil or plain feta cheese (optional)

Spring greens mix (optional)

1. Combine beans, artichokes, bell peppers, tomatoes, basil, oil, vinegar, garlic, mustard, black pepper and salt in large bowl; toss gently.

2. Fold in cheese, if desired. Let stand at least 10 minutes before serving. Serve on greens, if desired.

Charred Corn Salad

Makes 6 servings

3 tablespoons fresh lime juice

½ teaspoon salt

¼ cup olive oil

4 ears corn, kernels removed

⅔ cup canned black beans, rinsed
   and drained

½ cup chopped fresh cilantro

2 teaspoons minced seeded
   chipotle pepper (about
   1 canned chipotle pepper
   in adobo sauce)

1. Whisk lime juice and salt in small bowl; gradually whisk in oil until well blended.

2. Heat large skillet over medium-high heat. Cook corn in single layer 5 to 7 minutes or until browned and tender, stirring frequently. Transfer to large bowl; cool slightly.

3. Place beans in small microwavable bowl; microwave on HIGH 1 minute or until heated through. Add beans, cilantro and chipotle pepper to corn; mix well. Pour lime juice mixture over corn mixture; stir gently to coat.

Note: Place leftover chipotle peppers and sauce in a covered food storage container or resealable food storage bag and refrigerate or freeze.

soups

Vegetable and Red Lentil Soup

Makes 4 servings

1 can (about 14 ounces) vegetable broth

1 can (about 14 ounces) diced tomatoes

2 medium zucchini or yellow squash (or 1 of each), chopped

1 red or yellow bell pepper, chopped

½ cup thinly sliced carrots

½ cup dried red lentils, rinsed and sorted*

½ teaspoon salt

½ teaspoon sugar

¼ teaspoon black pepper

2 tablespoons chopped fresh basil or thyme

If red lentils are not available, substitute dried brown lentils.

1. Combine broth, tomatoes, zucchini, bell pepper, carrots, lentils, salt, sugar and black pepper in large saucepan. Bring to a boil over high heat. Reduce heat to medium-low; cover and simmer 30 minutes or until lentils and vegetables are tender.

2. Ladle into bowls; top with basil.

Black Bean Soup

Makes 4 to 6 servings

2 tablespoons vegetable oil

1 cup diced onion

1 stalk celery, diced

2 carrots, diced

½ small green bell pepper, diced

4 cloves garlic, minced

4 cans (about 15 ounces each) black beans, rinsed and drained, divided

4 cups vegetable broth, divided

2 tablespoons cider vinegar

2 teaspoons chili powder

½ teaspoon salt

½ teaspoon ground red pepper

½ teaspoon ground cumin

¼ teaspoon liquid smoke

Optional toppings: sour cream, chopped green onions and shredded Cheddar cheese

1. Heat oil in large saucepan or Dutch oven over medium-low heat. Add onion, celery, carrots, bell pepper and garlic; cook 10 minutes, stirring occasionally.

2. Combine half of beans and 1 cup broth in food processor or blender; process until smooth. Add to vegetables in saucepan.

3. Stir in remaining beans, remaining broth, vinegar, chili powder, salt, red pepper, cumin and liquid smoke; bring to a boil over high heat. Reduce heat to medium-low; cook 1 hour or until vegetables are tender and soup is thickened. Serve with desired toppings.

Lentil Soup

Makes 6 to 8 servings

2 tablespoons olive oil, divided

2 medium onions, chopped

1½ teaspoons salt

4 cloves garlic, minced

¼ cup tomato paste

1 teaspoon dried oregano

½ teaspoon dried basil

¼ teaspoon dried thyme

¼ teaspoon black pepper

½ cup dry sherry or white wine

8 cups vegetable broth

2 cups water

3 carrots, cut into ½-inch pieces

2 cups dried brown or green lentils, rinsed and sorted

1 cup chopped fresh parsley

1 tablespoon balsamic vinegar

1. Heat 1 tablespoon oil in large saucepan or Dutch oven over medium heat. Add onions; cook 10 minutes, stirring occasionally. Add remaining 1 tablespoon oil and salt; cook 10 minutes or until onions are golden brown, stirring frequently.

2. Add garlic; cook and stir 1 minute. Add tomato paste, oregano, basil, thyme and pepper; cook and stir 1 minute. Stir in sherry; cook 30 seconds, scraping up browned bits from bottom of saucepan.

3. Stir in broth, water, carrots and lentils; cover and bring to a boil over high heat. Reduce heat to medium-low; cook, partially covered, 30 minutes or until lentils are tender.

4. Remove from heat; stir in parsley and vinegar.

Mushroom Barley Soup

Makes 4 servings

2 tablespoons olive oil

1 package (8 ounces) sliced mushrooms

½ cup chopped onion

½ cup chopped carrots

1 clove garlic, minced

1 teaspoon dried thyme

¼ teaspoon salt

¼ teaspoon black pepper

¼ cup dry white wine

4 cups vegetable broth

¾ cup quick-cooking barley

1. Heat oil in large saucepan over medium-high heat. Add mushrooms, onion, carrots, garlic, thyme, salt and pepper; cook and stir 6 to 8 minutes or until mushrooms begin to brown. Add wine, stirring to scrape up browned bits from bottom of saucepan.

2. Stir in broth; bring to a boil over high heat. Stir in barley. Reduce heat to low; simmer, partially covered, 15 minutes or until barley is tender.

Lentil Vegetable Stew

Makes 8 servings

3 tablespoons vegetable oil

1 large onion, coarsely chopped

1 can (28 ounces) crushed tomatoes

2 cups water

1 tablespoon curry powder

1 tablespoon cider vinegar

1½ teaspoons salt

1½ teaspoons ground cumin

1½ teaspoons ground coriander

1 teaspoon ground ginger

1¼ cups dried brown or green lentils, rinsed and sorted

2 cups cauliflower florets

1 cup chopped red bell pepper

1 cup chopped yellow squash

1. Heat oil in large saucepan over medium heat. Add onion; cook and stir 5 minutes or until softened. Stir in tomatoes, water, curry powder, vinegar, salt, cumin, coriander and ginger. Stir in lentils; bring to a boil. Reduce heat to medium-low; simmer 35 to 40 minutes or until lentils begin to soften.

2. Add cauliflower, bell pepper and squash; cook 30 to 40 minutes or until vegetables and lentils are tender.

Greens, White Bean and Barley Soup

Makes 8 servings

2 tablespoons olive oil

1½ cups chopped onions

3 carrots, diced

2 cloves garlic, minced

1½ cups sliced mushrooms

6 cups vegetable broth

2 cups cooked barley

1 can (about 15 ounces) Great Northern beans, rinsed and drained

2 bay leaves

1 teaspoon sugar

1 teaspoon dried thyme

7 cups chopped stemmed collard greens (about 24 ounces)

1 tablespoon white wine vinegar

Hot pepper sauce

Red bell pepper strips (optional)

1. Heat oil in Dutch oven over medium heat. Add onions, carrots and garlic; cook and stir 3 minutes. Add mushrooms; cook and stir 5 minutes or until carrots are tender.

2. Add broth, barley, beans, bay leaves, sugar and thyme; bring to a boil over high heat. Reduce heat to medium-low; cover and simmer 5 minutes. Add greens; simmer 10 minutes. Remove and discard bay leaves. Stir in vinegar. Season with hot pepper sauce. Garnish with red bell peppers.

Navy Bean Vegetable Soup

Makes 8 servings

1 cup dried navy beans, rinsed and sorted

3 cups water

1 teaspoon salt, divided

1 pound leeks (about 2), cut into ½-inch pieces

2 cups sliced mushrooms

1½ cups thinly sliced carrots

12 ounces new potatoes or small red potatoes, cut into wedges

6 cups vegetable broth

1½ teaspoons dried thyme leaves

1 bay leaf

½ teaspoon black pepper

Chopped tomatoes

Crispy corn tortilla strips

1. Place beans in large saucepan. Add water. Bring to a boil over high heat. Cover and remove from heat. Let stand 30 minutes. Return to a boil over high heat. Reduce heat to low. Cover and simmer 30 minutes; stir in ½ teaspoon salt. Cover and simmer 1 hour more; drain.

2. Add leeks, mushrooms, carrots, potatoes, broth, thyme, bay leaf, remaining ½ teaspoon salt and pepper to Dutch oven. Bring to a boil over high heat. Reduce heat to low. Cover and simmer 25 minutes. Add beans and cook 5 minutes. Remove and discard bay leaf.

3. Ladle soup into shallow bowls; sprinkle with tomatoes and tortilla strips.

Chunky Italian Stew with White Beans

Makes 4 servings

1 teaspoon olive oil

2 green bell peppers, cut into ¾-inch pieces

1 yellow squash, cut into ¾-inch pieces

1 zucchini, cut into ¾-inch pieces

1 onion, cut into ¾-inch pieces

1 cup quartered mushrooms

1 can (about 15 ounces) navy beans, rinsed and drained

1 can (about 14 ounces) diced tomatoes

1 teaspoon dried oregano

¾ teaspoon salt

½ teaspoon sugar

½ teaspoon Italian seasoning

⅛ teaspoon red pepper flakes (optional)

¾ cup (3 ounces) shredded mozzarella cheese (optional)

1 tablespoon grated Parmesan cheese (optional)

1. Heat oil in Dutch oven or large saucepan over medium-high heat. Add bell peppers, squash, zucchini, onion and mushrooms; cook and stir 8 minutes or until onion is translucent.

2. Stir in beans, tomatoes, oregano, salt, sugar, Italian seasoning and red pepper flakes, if desired. Reduce heat; cover and simmer 15 minutes or until vegetables are tender, stirring once. Top with cheeses just before serving, if desired.

Roasted Butternut Squash Soup

Makes 4 servings

1 butternut squash (about 1½ pounds)

2 tablespoons olive oil, divided

⅔ cup chopped onion

2½ cups vegetable broth

1 Granny Smith apple, peeled and cubed

½ teaspoon salt

¼ teaspoon ground cinnamon

⅛ teaspoon ground nutmeg

⅛ teaspoon black pepper

¼ cup half-and-half (optional)

Toasted pumpkin seeds (pepitas)

1. Preheat oven to 400°F. Line baking sheet with foil. Peel squash; cut in half lengthwise. Remove and discard seeds and strings. Cut squash into 2-inch cubes; place on prepared baking sheet and drizzle with 1 tablespoon oil. Bake 12 minutes or until almost tender.

2. Meanwhile, heat remaining 1 tablespoon oil in large saucepan over medium heat. Add onion; cook and stir about 5 minutes or until softened and lightly browned. Add broth, apple and salt; bring to a boil over high heat. Reduce heat to low; cover and simmer 10 minutes.

3. Add squash; cover and simmer 5 minutes or until tender. Remove from heat.

4. Working in batches, process soup in blender or food processor until smooth (or use immersion blender). Return to saucepan; stir in cinnamon, nutmeg and pepper. Simmer, uncovered, 3 minutes. Stir in half-and-half, if desired. Sprinkle with pumpkin seeds.

Double Pea Soup

Makes 6 servings

1 tablespoon vegetable oil

1 onion, finely chopped

3 cloves garlic, minced

6 cups water

2 cups dried split peas

1 bay leaf

1 teaspoon ground mustard

1½ cups frozen green peas

1 teaspoon salt

¼ teaspoon black pepper

Sour cream (optional)

1. Heat oil in large saucepan or Dutch oven over medium-high heat. Add onion; cook and stir 5 minutes or until tender. Add garlic; cook and stir 1 minute. Add water, split peas, bay leaf and mustard; bring to a boil over high heat. Reduce heat to medium-low; cover and simmer 45 minutes or until split peas are tender, stirring occasionally.

2. Stir in green peas, salt and pepper; cover and simmer 10 minutes or until green peas are tender. Remove and discard bay leaf.

3. Working in batches, blend soup in blender or food processor until smooth (or use immersion blender). Serve with sour cream, if desired.

Sweet Potato-Peanut Soup

Makes 4 servings

1 tablespoon vegetable oil

1½ cups chopped onion

1 clove garlic, minced

2 teaspoons chili powder

1 teaspoon ground cumin

¼ teaspoon red pepper flakes

3 cups vegetable broth

1 can (about 14 ounces) diced tomatoes, undrained

8 ounces sweet potatoes, peeled and cut into ½-inch cubes

1 medium carrot, cut into ½-inch pieces

1 cup salted peanuts

1 tablespoon grated fresh ginger

¼ cup chopped fresh cilantro

1. Heat oil in large saucepan over medium-high heat. Add onion; cook and stir 5 minutes or until softened. Add garlic, chili powder, cumin and red pepper flakes; cook and stir 15 seconds.

2. Add broth, tomatoes, sweet potatoes and carrot; bring to a boil over high heat. Reduce heat to medium. Cover tightly; simmer 25 minutes or until vegetables are tender, stirring occasionally. Remove from heat. Stir in peanuts and ginger. Cool slightly.

3. Working in batches, process soup in blender or food processor until smooth (or use immersion blender). Return to saucepan. Heat over medium-high heat 2 minutes or until heated through. Sprinkle with cilantro just before serving.

grains

Quinoa and Mango Salad

Makes 4 to 6 servings

1 cup uncooked quinoa

2 cups water

2 cups cubed peeled mangoes (about 2 large mangoes)

½ cup sliced green onions

½ cup dried cranberries

2 tablespoons chopped fresh parsley

¼ cup olive oil

1 tablespoon plus 1½ teaspoons white wine vinegar

1 teaspoon Dijon mustard

½ teaspoon salt

⅛ teaspoon black pepper

1. Place quinoa in fine-mesh strainer; rinse well under cold water. Combine quinoa and 2 cups water in medium saucepan; bring to a boil over high heat. Reduce heat to low; cover and simmer about 15 minutes until quinoa is tender and water is absorbed. Stir quinoa; let stand, covered, 15 minutes. Transfer to large bowl; cover and refrigerate at least 1 hour.

2. Add mangoes, green onions, cranberries and parsley to quinoa; mix well.

3. Combine oil, vinegar, mustard, salt and pepper in small bowl; whisk until blended. Pour over quinoa mixture; mix until well blended.

Tip: This salad can be made several hours ahead and refrigerated. Allow it to stand at room temperature for at least 30 minutes before serving.

Chile and Lime Quinoa

Makes 4 servings

½ cup uncooked quinoa

1 cup water

1 jalapeño pepper, seeded and minced

2 tablespoons finely chopped green onion

2 tablespoons olive oil

1 tablespoon fresh lime juice

¼ teaspoon salt

¼ teaspoon ground cumin

¼ teaspoon chili powder

⅛ teaspoon black pepper

1. Place quinoa in fine-mesh strainer; rinse well under cold water. Combine quinoa and 1 cup water in medium saucepan; bring to a boil over medium-high heat. Reduce heat to low; cover and simmer about 15 minutes or until quinoa is tender and water is absorbed. Let stand, covered, 5 minutes.

2. Stir jalapeño pepper, green onion, oil, lime juice, salt, cumin, chili powder and black pepper into quinoa. Fluff mixture with fork. Serve warm or at room temperature.

Citrus Rice Salad

Makes 4 servings

½ cup uncooked brown rice

1 stalk celery, chopped

1 orange, peeled, seeded and cut into ½-inch pieces

1 tablespoon orange juice

1½ teaspoons canola oil

1½ teaspoons white wine vinegar

½ teaspoon curry powder

¼ teaspoon salt

⅛ teaspoon black pepper

2 tablespoons minced fresh chives

2 tablespoons sliced almonds

1. Cook rice according to package directions. Cool to room temperature. Place in serving bowl. Stir in celery and orange.

2. Whisk orange juice, oil, vinegar, curry powder, salt and pepper in small bowl until well blended. Pour over rice mixture; mix well. Stir in chives; sprinkle with almonds just before serving.

Wheat Berry Apple Salad

Makes 6 to 8 servings (about 6 cups)

1 cup uncooked wheat berries
   (whole wheat kernels)

½ teaspoon salt

2 apples (1 red and 1 green)

½ cup dried cranberries

⅓ cup chopped walnuts

1 stalk celery, chopped

Grated peel and juice of
   1 medium orange

2 tablespoons rice wine vinegar

1½ tablespoons chopped fresh
   mint

1. Place wheat berries and salt in large saucepan; cover with 1 inch of water.* Bring to a boil. Stir and reduce heat to low. Cover and cook 45 minutes to 1 hour or until wheat berries are tender but chewy, stirring occasionally. (Add additional water if wheat berries become dry during cooking.) Drain and let cool. (Refrigerate for up to 4 days if not using immediately.)

2. Cut unpeeled apples into bite-size pieces. Combine wheat berries, apples, cranberries, walnuts, celery, orange peel, orange juice, vinegar and mint in large bowl. Cover; refrigerate at least 1 hour to allow flavors to blend.

To cut cooking time by 20 to 30 minutes, soak wheat berries in water overnight. Drain and cover with 1 inch of fresh water before cooking.

Broccoli, White Bean and Bulgur Gratin

Makes 4 servings

⅔ cup uncooked bulgur
  Boiling water
4 cups small broccoli florets
1 can (about 15 ounces) Great Northern beans, rinsed and drained
1 tablespoon olive oil
½ teaspoon salt
½ teaspoon dried thyme
⅛ teaspoon black pepper
1 cup vegetable broth
¾ cup (3 ounces) shredded mozzarella cheese or mozzarella-style vegan cheese alternative

1. Place bulgur in large bowl; add enough boiling water to cover by 1 inch. Let stand 25 minutes or until bulgur is tender and water is absorbed.

2. Preheat oven to 375°F. Spray 2-quart baking dish with nonstick cooking spray.

3. Steam broccoli in steamer basket over boiling water 4 minutes or until tender.

4. Combine bulgur, broccoli, beans, oil, salt, thyme and pepper in prepared baking dish; gently combine and spread into even layer. Pour broth over mixture; sprinkle evenly with cheese.

5. Bake 30 minutes or until golden brown and cheese is melted. Let stand 5 minutes before serving.

Brown Rice and Vegetable Stuffed Squash

Makes 4 servings

2 large acorn or golden acorn squash (about 1½ pounds each)

1 cup uncooked quick-cooking brown rice

2 cups broccoli florets, chopped

½ teaspoon salt

½ teaspoon black pepper

¼ cup chopped almonds, toasted*

¾ cup (3 ounces) shredded sharp Cheddar or smoked Gouda cheese

To toast almonds, spread in single layer in small heavy skillet. Cook over medium heat 1 to 2 minutes or until lightly browned, stirring frequently. Remove from skillet; cool before using.

1. Preheat oven to 375°F. Cut squash in half crosswise; scrape out and discard seeds. Trim off stems and a small portion of rounded ends to allow squash to stand when filled.

2. Place squash halves cut side down on microwavable plate; microwave on HIGH 12 to 15 minutes, or until almost tender when pierced. Place squash halves in 13×9-inch baking pan, cut side up. Cover; let stand 3 minutes or until ready to fill.

3. Meanwhile, cook rice according to package directions, adding broccoli, salt and pepper during last 5 minutes of cooking. Stir in almonds.

4. Mound rice mixture into squash, overflowing into pan if necessary; sprinkle with cheese. Bake 20 to 25 minutes or until squash is tender and cheese is melted.

Pumpkin Risotto

Makes 4 servings

4 cups vegetable broth

5 whole fresh sage leaves

¼ teaspoon ground nutmeg

2 tablespoons butter or vegan plant butter

1 tablespoon olive oil

1 onion, finely chopped

2 cloves garlic, minced

1½ cups uncooked arborio rice

½ cup dry white wine

1 teaspoon salt

Black pepper

1 can (15 ounces) solid-pack pumpkin

½ cup shredded Parmesan cheese (optional)

2 tablespoons chopped fresh sage, divided

¼ cup toasted pumpkin seeds (pepitas) or chopped toasted walnuts or pecans

1. Combine broth, whole sage leaves and nutmeg in small saucepan; bring to a boil over high heat. Reduce heat to low to maintain a simmer.

2. Heat butter and oil in large saucepan over medium-high heat. Add onion; cook and stir 5 minutes or until softened. Add garlic; cook and stir 30 seconds. Add rice; cook 2 to 3 minutes or until rice appears translucent, stirring frequently to coat with butter. Add wine, salt and pepper; cook until most of liquid is absorbed.

3. Add broth mixture, ½ cup at a time, stirring frequently until broth is absorbed before adding next ½ cup (discard whole sage leaves). Stir in pumpkin when about 1 cup broth remains. Add remaining broth; cook until rice is al dente, stirring constantly.

4. Remove from heat; stir in cheese, if desired, and 1 tablespoon chopped sage. Cover and let stand 5 minutes. Top each serving with 1 tablespoon pumpkin seeds and remaining 1 tablespoon chopped sage.

Cheesy Baked Barley

Makes 4 servings

4 cups water

1 cup uncooked pearl barley

1 teaspoon salt, divided

2 tablespoons olive oil

1 onion, chopped

1 cup chopped zucchini

1 cup chopped red bell pepper

1 tablespoon all-purpose flour

1½ cups milk

2 cups (8 ounces) shredded Italian or Mexican blend cheese, divided

2 tablespoons Dijon mustard

Black pepper

1. Bring water to a boil in small saucepan. Add barley and ½ teaspoon salt. Reduce heat; cover and simmer 45 minutes or until barley is tender and water is absorbed (drain any remaining water).

2. Preheat oven to 375°F. Spray 2-quart baking dish with nonstick cooking spray.

3. Heat oil in large saucepan over medium heat. Add onion, zucchini and bell pepper; cook and stir 5 to 7 minutes or until soft.

4. Stir in flour and remaining ½ teaspoon salt; cook 1 minute. Gradually stir in milk; cook and stir 2 to 3 minutes or until slightly thickened. Remove from heat. Add barley, 1½ cups cheese and mustard; stir until cheese is melted. Season with black pepper. Spread mixture in prepared baking dish; sprinkle with remaining ½ cup cheese.

5. Bake 20 minutes or until hot. Preheat broiler. Broil casserole 1 to 2 minutes or until cheese is lightly browned.

beans

Black Bean and Rice Stuffed Poblano Peppers

Makes 4 servings

4   large poblano peppers

1   can (about 15 ounces) black beans, rinsed and drained

1   cup cooked brown rice

⅔   cup chunky salsa

¾   cup (3 ounces) shredded Cheddar cheese or pepper-jack cheese or Cheddar-style vegan cheese alternative, divided

1. Preheat oven to 375°F. Spray shallow baking pan with nonstick cooking spray.

2. Cut thin slice from one side of each pepper. Chop pepper slices; set aside. Bring medium saucepan of water to a boil. Add whole peppers; cook 6 minutes. Drain and rinse with cold water. Remove and discard seeds and membranes.

3. Stir together beans, rice, salsa, chopped pepper and ½ cup cheese in small bowl. Spoon into peppers, mounding mixture. Place peppers in prepared pan. Cover with foil. Bake 12 to 15 minutes or until heated through.

4. Sprinkle with remaining ¼ cup cheese. Bake 2 minutes or until cheese melts.

Marinated Bean and Vegetable Salad

Makes 4 to 6 servings

¼ cup orange juice

3 tablespoons white wine vinegar

1 tablespoon canola oil

2 cloves garlic, minced

1 can (about 15 ounces) Great Northern beans, rinsed and drained

1 can (about 15 ounces) kidney beans, rinsed and drained

¼ cup coarsely chopped red cabbage

¼ cup chopped red onion

¼ cup chopped green bell pepper

¼ cup chopped red bell pepper

¼ cup sliced celery

Salt and black pepper

1. Combine orange juice, vinegar, oil and garlic in small jar with tight-fitting lid; shake well.

2. Combine beans, cabbage, onion, bell peppers and celery in large bowl. Pour dressing over bean mixture; toss to coat. Season with salt and black pepper.

3. Refrigerate, covered, 1 to 2 hours to allow flavors to blend. Toss before serving.

Orzo, Black Bean and Edamame Salad

Makes 4 servings

⅔ cup uncooked orzo pasta

¾ cup frozen shelled edamame

¾ cup diced carrots

¾ cup canned black beans, rinsed and drained

½ cup diced green bell pepper

2 tablespoons lime juice

1 tablespoon olive oil

¼ teaspoon salt

⅛ teaspoon black pepper

2 tablespoons finely chopped fresh cilantro

2 tablespoons grated Parmesan cheese (optional)

1. Cook orzo in medium saucepan of boiling salted water according to package directions until tender, adding edamame and carrots about 5 minutes before end of cooking time. Drain and place in large bowl; add beans and bell pepper.

2. Whisk lime juice, oil, salt and black pepper in small bowl; pour over salad. Add cilantro and cheese, if desired; toss gently to blend. Serve lukewarm or at room temperature.

Brown Rice with Chickpeas, Spinach and Feta

Makes 4 servings

1   tablespoon olive oil

½   cup diced celery

½   cup uncooked instant brown rice

1   can (about 15 ounces) chickpeas, rinsed and drained

1   package (10 ounces) frozen chopped spinach, thawed and squeezed dry

1   clove garlic, minced

1   teaspoon Greek or Italian seasoning

¼   teaspoon salt

⅛   teaspoon black pepper

2   cups water or vegetable broth

½   cup (2 ounces) crumbled feta cheese

1   tablespoon lemon juice

1. Heat oil in large skillet over medium-high heat. Add celery; cook 4 minutes or until lightly browned in spots, stirring occasionally.

2. Add rice, chickpeas, spinach, garlic, Greek seasoning, salt and pepper; stir in water. Stir to combine. Cover and bring to a boil over medium-high heat. Reduce heat to low; simmer 12 minutes or until rice is tender. Remove from heat; stir in cheese and lemon juice.

Mediterranean Barley-Bean Salad

Makes 4 servings

⅔ cup uncooked pearl barley

3 cups cut asparagus (1-inch pieces)

2 cans (about 15 ounces each) dark red kidney beans, rinsed and drained

2 tablespoons chopped fresh mint

¼ cup lemon juice

¼ cup Italian salad dressing

Salt and black pepper

¼ cup dry-roasted sunflower seeds

1. Cook barley according to package directions. Add asparagus during last 5 minutes of cooking. Drain and place in large bowl. Cover and refrigerate at least 2 hours.

2. Stir beans and mint into barley mixture. Whisk lemon juice and salad dressing in small bowl until well blended. Add to barley mixture; toss to coat. Season with salt and pepper. Sprinkle with sunflower seeds.

Black Bean and Mushroom Chilaquiles

Makes 6 servings

2 tablespoons olive oil

1 medium onion, chopped

1 green bell pepper, chopped

1 jalapeño or serrano pepper, seeded and minced

1 package (8 ounces) white mushrooms, cut into quarters

2 cans (about 15 ounces each) black beans, rinsed and drained

1 can (about 14 ounces) diced tomatoes

1½ teaspoons ground cumin

1½ teaspoons dried oregano

Salt and black pepper

1 cup (4 ounces) shredded Cheddar cheese or Cheddar-style vegan cheese alternative, plus additional for garnish

6 cups tortilla chips

1. Heat oil in large skillet over medium heat. Add onion, bell pepper and jalapeño pepper; cook and stir 5 minutes or until softened. Add mushrooms; cook and stir 6 to 8 minutes or until mushrooms are browned and have released their liquid.

2. Stir in beans, tomatoes, cumin and oregano. Reduce heat to medium; cook 10 minutes, stirring occasionally. Season with salt and black pepper. Stir in 1 cup cheese until melted.

3. Coarsely crush tortilla chips. Top with black bean mixture and sprinkle with additional cheese.

Confetti Black Beans

Makes 6 servings

1 tablespoon olive oil

1 medium onion, chopped

¼ cup chopped red bell pepper

¼ cup chopped yellow bell pepper

2 cloves garlic, minced

1 jalapeño pepper, finely chopped

1 large tomato, seeded and chopped

1 teaspoon salt

⅛ teaspoon black pepper

2 cans (about 15 ounces each) black beans, rinsed and drained

Hot pepper sauce (optional)

1. Heat oil in large nonstick skillet over medium heat. Add onion, bell peppers, garlic and jalapeño pepper; cook and stir 8 to 10 minutes or until onion is translucent. Add tomato, salt and black pepper; cook and stir 5 minutes.

2. Reduce heat to medium-low. Add beans; cook 15 minutes, stirring frequently. Serve with hot pepper sauce, if desired.

Greek Lentil Salad with Feta Vinaigrette

Makes 2 to 4 servings

4 cups water

1 cup dried brown or green lentils, rinsed and sorted

1 bay leaf

¼ cup chopped green onions

1 stalk celery, chopped

1 cup grape tomatoes, halved

¼ cup (1 ounce) crumbled feta cheese

2 tablespoons olive oil

1 tablespoon white wine vinegar

½ teaspoon dried thyme

½ teaspoon dried oregano

½ teaspoon salt

¼ teaspoon black pepper

1. Combine water, lentils and bay leaf in medium saucepan. Bring to a boil. Reduce heat to medium-low; partially cover and cook 40 minutes or until lentils are tender but not mushy.

2. Drain lentils; remove and discard bay leaf. Place lentils in serving bowl; stir in green onions, celery and tomatoes.

3. Combine cheese, oil, vinegar, thyme, oregano, salt and pepper in small bowl. Pour over salad; gently stir until blended. Let stand at least 10 minutes before serving to allow flavors to blend.

Bean Salad with Chipotle Chile Dressing

Makes 4 servings

1 can (about 15 ounces) kidney beans, rinsed and drained

1 cup cherry or grape tomatoes, halved

1 green bell pepper, chopped

¼ cup finely chopped green onions

1 jalapeño pepper, minced

½ cup (2 ounces) shredded Monterey Jack cheese (optional)

1 tablespoon vegetable broth

1 tablespoon tomato paste

2 teaspoons canola oil

1 teaspoon white wine vinegar

¼ teaspoon salt

¼ teaspoon black pepper

¼ teaspoon ground cumin

⅛ teaspoon chipotle chili powder

1. Combine beans, tomatoes, bell pepper, green onions, jalapeño pepper and cheese, if desired, in large bowl; mix well.

2. Combine broth, tomato paste, oil, vinegar, salt, black pepper, cumin and chile powder in a cup. Stir well. Pour over salad; mix well. Let stand 5 minutes for flavors to blend.

Note: This salad makes a great filing for quesadillas, tacos or burritos.

Puerto Rican Sofrito Beans with Rice

Makes 8 servings

2 cups water

1 cup uncooked long grain rice

1¼ teaspoons salt, divided

½ cup finely chopped red and/or yellow bell pepper (optional)

¾ cup chopped fresh cilantro, divided

1 green bell pepper, cut into quarters

1 small onion, cut into quarters

2 tablespoons olive oil

1 tablespoon minced garlic

1 teaspoon ground cumin

¼ teaspoon ground red pepper

2 medium tomatoes, chopped

1 can (8 ounces) tomato sauce

1 can (about 15 ounces) black beans, rinsed and drained

1 can (about 15 ounces) red beans, rinsed and drained

1. Combine water, rice and ¾ teaspoon salt in medium saucepan. Bring to a boil over high heat. Reduce heat to low; cover and simmer 20 minutes or until water is absorbed. Stir in red bell pepper, if desired, and ¼ cup cilantro.

2. Meanwhile, place green bell pepper, onion and remaining ½ cup cilantro in food processor; process until finely chopped.

3. Heat oil in large skillet over medium-high heat. Add bell pepper mixture, garlic, remaining ½ teaspoon salt, cumin and ground red pepper; cook and stir 5 minutes. Stir in tomatoes and tomato sauce; cook 5 minutes. Stir in beans; cook 5 minutes. Serve bean mixture with rice.

pasta

Ziti Ratatouille

Makes 6 to 8 servings

- 1 jar (about 24 ounces) marinara sauce
- 2 cans (about 14 ounces each) diced tomatoes with garlic and onions
- 1 large eggplant, peeled and cut into ½-inch cubes (about 1½ pounds)
- 2 medium zucchini, cut into ½-inch cubes
- 1 green or red bell pepper, cut into ½-inch pieces
- 1 onion, chopped
- 4 cloves garlic, minced
- 8 ounces uncooked ziti pasta
- 1 can (6 ounces) pitted black olives, drained

  Lemon juice (optional)

  Shaved Parmesan cheese (optional)

1. Combine marinara sauce, tomatoes, eggplant, zucchini, bell pepper, onion and garlic in Dutch oven or large saucepan. Bring to a simmer over medium-high heat. Reduce heat to low; cover and cook 20 to 30 minutes or until vegetables are tender.

2. Meanwhile, cook pasta in large saucepan of boiling salted water according to package directions until al dente. Drain; stir into vegetable mixture with olives. Drizzle with lemon juice, if desired. Garnish with cheese.

Fire-Roasted Tomatoes with Gemelli Pasta

Makes 4 servings

4 pounds plum tomatoes (about 30 tomatoes)

12 ounces uncooked gemelli, penne, or fusilli pasta

1 shallot, sliced

½ to 1 jalapeño pepper, seeded and coarsely chopped

1 clove garlic, sliced

20 large fresh basil leaves

1 tablespoon olive oil

¾ teaspoon salt

⅛ teaspoon black pepper

½ cup crumbled goat cheese, feta or blue cheese

1. Prepare grill for direct cooking.

2. Cut tomatoes in half lengthwise; remove seeds. Grill tomatoes, skin-side down, over medium-high heat about 5 minutes or until skin is blackened and tomatoes are very tender. When tomatoes are cool enough to handle, remove skins.

3. Meanwhile, cook pasta in large saucepan of boiling salted water according to package directions until al dente. Drain; return to saucepan and keep warm.

4. Combine shallot, jalapeño pepper and garlic in food processor; process until finely chopped. Add tomatoes, basil, oil, salt and black pepper; process until well blended. Pour sauce over pasta. Cook and stir 1 minute over medium-high heat.

5. Remove from heat; stir in cheese. Serve immediately.

Note: Tomatoes can be broiled rather than grilled. Preheat broiler; prepare tomatoes as directed in step 2. Place tomatoes, cut side down, on broiler pan. Broil tomatoes 5 minutes or until skin is blackened and tomatoes are very tender.

Fusilli Pizzaiolo

Makes 6 to 8 servings

1 package (16 ounces) uncooked fusilli or rotini pasta

¼ cup olive oil

8 ounces mushrooms, sliced

1 red bell pepper, chopped

1 green bell pepper, chopped

1 yellow bell pepper, chopped

3 large shallots, chopped

10 green onions, chopped

1 large sweet onion, chopped

8 cloves garlic, minced

½ cup chopped fresh basil *or* 2 teaspoons dried basil

2 tablespoons chopped fresh oregano *or* 1 teaspoon dried oregano

Dash red pepper flakes

4 cups canned or fresh tomatoes, undrained, chopped

Salt and black pepper

1. Cook pasta in large saucepan of boiling salted water according to package directions until al dente. Drain and return to saucepan; keep warm.

2. Heat oil in large skillet over medium-high heat. Add mushrooms, bell peppers, shallots, green onions, sweet onion, garlic, chopped basil, oregano and red pepper flakes; cook and stir 10 minutes or until onion is lightly browned.

3. Add tomatoes with juice; bring to a boil. Reduce heat to low; simmer, uncovered, 20 minutes. Season with salt and black pepper.

4. Add pasta to sauce; toss to coat.

Roasted Fennel and Spaghetti

Makes 2 to 4 servings

2 bulbs fennel, trimmed, cored and sliced ¼ inch thick

2 carrots, quartered lengthwise

1 tablespoon plus 2 teaspoons olive oil, divided

Salt and black pepper

1 cup fresh bread crumbs

2 cloves garlic, minced

8 ounces uncooked vermicelli or spaghetti

2 tablespoons fresh lemon juice

2 tablespoons chopped fresh oregano

1. Preheat oven to 400°F. Place fennel and carrots on sheet pan. Drizzle with 1 teaspoon oil and season with salt and pepper (about ¼ teaspoon each). Toss to coat; spread in single layer.

2. Bake 30 minutes or until vegetables are tender and well browned, stirring once or twice. When carrots are cool enough to handle, cut diagonally into 1-inch pieces.

3. Meanwhile, heat 1 tablespoon oil in medium skillet over medium heat. Add bread crumbs and garlic; cook and stir about 3 minutes or until bread is toasted. Transfer to small bowl; season with ¼ teaspoon salt.

4. Cook pasta in large saucepan of boiling salted water according to package directions until al dente. Drain and return to saucepan. Stir in lemon juice and remaining 1 teaspoon oil. Divide pasta among serving bowls. Top with vegetables, bread crumbs and oregano.

Tip: To make fresh bread crumbs, place stale or soft bread in a food processor and pulse until small pea-size pieces form.

Spaghetti with Pesto Tofu Squares

Makes 4 servings

1 package (about 14 ounces) extra firm tofu

¼ to ½ cup prepared pesto

8 ounces uncooked spaghetti

1 jar (24 ounces) marinara sauce

½ cup shredded Parmesan cheese (optional)

¼ cup pine nuts, toasted*

To toast pine nuts, spread in single layer in small heavy skillet. Cook over medium heat 1 to 2 minutes or until lightly browned, stirring frequently. Remove from skillet; cool before using.

1. Preheat oven to 350°F. Spray shallow baking dish with nonstick cooking spray.

2. Cut tofu into 1-inch cubes. Combine tofu and pesto in medium bowl; stir gently to coat. Arrange in prepared baking dish. Bake 15 minutes.

3. Meanwhile, cook pasta in large saucepan of boiling salted water according to package directions until al dente; drain and return to saucepan. Add marinara sauce; toss to coat. Cover and cook 5 minutes over low heat or until hot.

4. Divide spaghetti among four plates; top with tofu cubes. Sprinkle with cheese, if desired, and pine nuts.

Zucchini and Mushroom Lasagna with Tofu

Makes 4 to 6 servings

1 tablespoon olive oil

1 cup thinly sliced onions

1 package (8 ounces) sliced mushrooms

2 small zucchini, thinly sliced

½ teaspoon black pepper, divided

½ (14-ounce) package silken tofu

1 egg

¼ teaspoon salt

1 jar (26 ounces) spicy red pepper pasta sauce

9 uncooked no-boil lasagna noodles

2 cups (8 ounces) shredded Italian cheese blend

¼ cup shredded Parmesan cheese

1. Preheat oven to 350°F. Spray 9-inch square baking dish with nonstick cooking spray.

2. Heat oil in large skillet. Add onions; cook and stir 2 minutes. Add mushrooms, zucchini and ¼ teaspoon pepper; cook and stir 8 minutes or until softened.

3. Meanwhile, combine tofu, egg, salt and remaining ¼ teaspoon pepper in medium bowl; mix until smooth.

4. Spread ½ cup pasta sauce over bottom of prepared dish. Arrange 3 noodles over sauce. Layer one third each vegetable mixture, tofu mixture, pasta sauce and Italian cheese blend. Repeat layers twice. Cover with foil.

5. Bake 1 hour. Remove foil; sprinkle with Parmesan cheese. Bake, uncovered, 15 minutes or until cheese is browned. Let stand 15 minutes before serving.

Peanut-Sauced Pasta

Makes 6 servings

⅓ cup vegetable broth

3 tablespoons creamy peanut butter

2 tablespoons seasoned rice vinegar

2 tablespoons soy sauce

½ teaspoon red pepper flakes

8 ounces uncooked multigrain linguine

1½ pounds fresh asparagus, cut into 1-inch pieces (4 cups)

⅓ cup dry-roasted peanuts, chopped

1. Whisk broth, peanut butter, vinegar, soy sauce and red pepper flakes in small saucepan until smooth. Cook over low heat until heated through, stirring frequently. Keep warm.

2. Cook pasta in large saucepan of boiling salted water according to package directions until al dente. Add asparagus to saucepan during last 5 minutes of cooking. Drain pasta and asparagus; toss with peanut sauce. Sprinkle with peanuts.

Pasta with Onions and Goat Cheese

Makes 8 servings

2 teaspoons olive oil

4 cups thinly sliced sweet onions

¾ cup (3 ounces) crumbled goat cheese

¼ cup milk

6 ounces uncooked campanelle or farfalle pasta

1 clove garlic, minced

2 tablespoons dry white wine or vegetable broth

1½ teaspoons chopped fresh sage *or* ½ teaspoon dried sage

½ teaspoon salt

¼ teaspoon black pepper

¼ cup chopped toasted walnuts

1. Heat oil in large skillet over medium heat. Add onions; cook about 20 to 25 minutes or until golden and caramelized, stirring occasionally.

2. Combine cheese and milk in small bowl; stir until well blended. Set aside.

3. Cook pasta in large saucepan of boiling salted water according to package directions until al dente. Drain; return to saucepan and keep warm.

4. Add garlic to onions in skillet; cook about 3 minutes or until softened. Add wine, sage, salt and pepper; cook until liquid has evaporated. Remove from heat. Add pasta and cheese mixture; stir until cheese is melted. Sprinkle with walnuts.

Rotini with Spinach, Beans and Romano Cheese

Makes 6 servings

8 ounces uncooked multigrain or whole wheat rotini

8 cups fresh spinach, stemmed and leaves torn

1 can (about 15 ounces) cannellini or Great Northern beans, rinsed and drained

½ cup shredded or grated Romano cheese

2 tablespoons olive oil

2 cloves garlic, minced

¼ teaspoon salt

¼ teaspoon black pepper

1. Cook pasta in large saucepan of boiling salted water according to package directions until al dente. Drain; place in large bowl.

2. Add spinach, beans, cheese, oil, garlic, salt and pepper; mix well.

Spaghetti with Creamy Tomato-Pepper Sauce

Makes 6 servings

1 package (16 ounces) uncooked regular or whole wheat spaghetti

2 tablespoons olive oil

1 small onion, chopped

2 tablespoons minced garlic

1 large red bell pepper, chopped

2 large tomatoes, seeded and chopped (about 3 cups)

½ cup grated Parmesan cheese

¼ cup half-and-half

½ teaspoon salt

½ teaspoon black pepper

1. Cook pasta in large saucepan of boiling salted water according to package directions until al dente. Drain and return to saucepan; keep warm.

2. Meanwhile, heat oil in large skillet over medium heat. Add onion and garlic; cook and stir 5 minutes or until onion is soft. (Add a little water if mixture seems dry.) Add bell pepper; cook 4 minutes or until pepper is crisp-tender. Stir in tomatoes.

3. Remove from heat; let cool 2 minutes. Return skillet to heat. Gradually stir in cheese, half-and-half, salt and black pepper. Reduce heat to low; cook 5 minutes or until heated through. Serve over spaghetti.

Southwestern Corn and Pasta Casserole

Makes 4 servings

- 2 tablespoons vegetable oil
- 1 onion, chopped
- 1 red bell pepper, chopped
- 1 jalapeño pepper, seeded and minced
- 1 clove garlic, minced
- 1 cup sliced mushrooms
- 2 cups frozen corn
- ½ teaspoon salt
- ¼ teaspoon ground cumin
- ¼ teaspoon chili powder
- 4 ounces whole wheat elbow macaroni, cooked and drained
- 1½ cups milk
- 1 tablespoon butter
- 1 tablespoon all-purpose flour
- 1 cup (4 ounces) shredded Monterey Jack cheese with chiles
- 1 slice whole wheat bread, cut or torn into ½-inch pieces

1. Preheat oven to 350°F. Grease 3-quart baking dish.

2. Heat oil in large skillet over medium-high heat. Add onion, bell pepper, jalapeño pepper and garlic; cook and stir 5 minutes. Add mushrooms; cook and stir 5 minutes. Add corn, salt, cumin and chili powder. Reduce heat to low; simmer 5 minutes or until corn thaws. Stir in macaroni; remove from heat.

3. Bring milk to a simmer in small saucepan over medium heat. Melt butter in large saucepan over medium heat; whisk in flour until smooth paste forms. Gradually whisk in milk. Cook and stir over medium-low heat 5 to 7 minutes or until slightly thickened. Gradually stir in cheese by handfuls; cook and stir over low heat until cheese melts. Stir macaroni mixture into cheese sauce; mix well.

4. Spoon into prepared baking dish. Sprinkle bread pieces over casserole. Bake 20 to 25 minutes or until bubbly. Let stand 5 minutes before serving.

Linguine with Sun-Dried Tomato Pesto

Makes 4 servings

8 ounces uncooked linguini or angel hair pasta

½ cup sun-dried tomatoes

½ cup loosely packed fresh basil leaves

2 tablespoons olive oil

1½ tablespoons grated Parmesan cheese

1 teaspoon dried oregano

1 clove garlic, minced

Salt and black pepper

1. Cook pasta in large saucepan of boiling salted water according to package directions for al dente. Drain and return to saucepan; keep warm.

2. Meanwhile, combine sun-dried tomatoes and ½ cup hot water in small bowl; soak 3 to 5 minutes or until tomatoes are soft and pliable. Drain; reserve liquid.

3. Combine tomatoes, basil, oil, cheese, oregano and garlic in food processor or blender. Process, adding enough reserved liquid, until mixture is of medium to thick sauce consistency. Season to taste with salt and pepper. Spoon over pasta and toss to coat; serve immediately.

sandwiches

Eggplant and Feta Stuffed Pitas

Makes 6 servings

1 tablespoon olive oil

1 cup diced onion

2½ cups diced eggplant

1 clove garlic, minced

1 cup grape tomatoes, quartered

¼ cup chopped fresh basil

3 whole wheat pita breads, warmed and halved

¼ cup balsamic vinaigrette salad dressing

¾ cup (3 ounces) crumbled feta cheese

1. Heat oil in large skillet over medium-high heat. Add onion; cook and stir 2 minutes. Add eggplant; cook and stir 4 to 6 minutes or until beginning to lightly brown. Add garlic; cook 15 seconds, stirring constantly. Add tomatoes; cook 2 minutes or just until tomatoes are tender.

2. Remove from heat; stir in basil. Cover; let stand 3 minutes to blend flavors. To serve, spoon vegetables into each pita half. Drizzle balsamic vinaigrette on top. Sprinkle with cheese.

Portobello Provolone Panini

Makes 4 servings

6 to 8 ounces sliced portobello mushrooms

⅓ cup plus 1 tablespoon olive oil, divided

3 tablespoons balsamic vinegar

1 clove garlic, minced

½ teaspoon salt

¼ teaspoon black pepper

1 loaf (16 ounces) ciabatta or Italian bread

8 ounces sliced provolone cheese or provolone-style vegan cheese alternative

¼ cup chopped fresh basil

8 ounces plum tomatoes, thinly sliced

3 tablespoons whole grain Dijon mustard

1. Place mushrooms, ⅓ cup oil, vinegar, garlic, salt and pepper in large resealable food storage bag. Seal tightly; shake to coat mushrooms evenly. Let stand 15 minutes, turning frequently. (Mushrooms may be prepared up to 24 hours in advance; refrigerate and turn occasionally.)

2. Preheat indoor grill or panini press. Brush both sides of bread with remaining 1 tablespoon oil; cut bread in half lengthwise.

3. Arrange mushrooms evenly over bottom half of bread; drizzle with some of remaining marinade. Top with cheese, basil and tomatoes. Spread mustard over cut side of remaining half of bread; place over tomatoes. Cut sandwich into four equal pieces.

4. Grill each sandwich 8 minutes or until cheese is melted and bread is golden brown. Wrap each sandwich tightly in foil to keep warm or serve at room temperature.

Tip: If you don't have an indoor grill or panini press, cook sandwiches in a skillet over medium heat. Weigh down sandwiches with another heavy skillet, a clean heavy can or a brick wrapped in foil.

Artichoke-Chickpea Pita Sandwiches

Makes 4 servings

1 cup plain yogurt

1 tablespoon chopped fresh cilantro

2 cloves garlic, minced

1 teaspoon lemon juice

1 can (about 15 ounces) chickpeas, rinsed and drained

1 can (14 ounces) artichoke hearts, rinsed, drained and coarsely chopped

1½ cups thinly sliced cucumber (halved lengthwise and thinly sliced)

½ cup shredded carrot

½ cup chopped green onions

Salt and black pepper

4 whole wheat pita breads, cut in half

1. Combine yogurt, cilantro, garlic and lemon juice in small bowl; mix well.

2. Combine chickpeas, artichoke hearts, cucumber, carrot and green onions in medium bowl. Stir in yogurt mixture until well blended. Season with salt and pepper. Divide mixture among pita halves.

Chickpea Wraps

Makes 4 servings

¼ cup ketchup

1 tablespoon red wine vinegar

1 teaspoon dried fines herbes*

1 teaspoon Dijon mustard

⅛ teaspoon black pepper

1 can (about 15 ounces) chickpeas, rinsed and drained

1 cup sliced mushrooms

8 cherry tomatoes, quartered

½ cup shredded carrot

½ cup (2 ounces) shredded Swiss cheese (optional)

4 large (10-inch) flour tortillas

8 lettuce leaves

Fines herbes is a combination of herbs commonly used in Mediterranean cooking. You can substitute ¼ teaspoon each: dried parsley flakes, dried chervil, dried tarragon and freeze-dried chives.

1. Combine ketchup, vinegar, fines herbes, mustard and pepper in medium bowl. Stir in chickpeas, mushrooms, tomatoes, carrot and cheese, if desired. Cover and refrigerate until ready to serve.

2. Line tortillas with lettuce. Top evenly with chickpea mixture. Roll up tortilla to enclose filling.

Waffled Caprese Panini

Makes 2 servings

- 2 tablespoons olive oil
- 4 slices Italian bread
- 2 ounces fresh mozzarella cheese, cut into slices *or* ½ cup shredded mozzarella cheese or mozzarella-style vegan cheese alternative
- 2 plum tomatoes, sliced
- 4 fresh basil leaves
- 8 pitted kalamata olives, cut in half

1. Preheat waffle maker to medium.

2. Brush oil on both sides of bread slices. Top two slices of bread with cheese, tomatoes, basil, olives and remaining bread slices.

3. Place sandwiches, one at a time, in waffle maker; close while pressing down slightly. Cook 2 minutes or until bread is golden brown and cheese is melted.

Avocado Toast

Makes 2 servings

½ cup thawed frozen peas

2 teaspoons lemon juice

1 teaspoon minced fresh tarragon

¼ teaspoon plus ⅛ teaspoon salt, divided

⅛ teaspoon black pepper

1 teaspoon olive oil

1 tablespoon raw pumpkin seeds (pepitas)

4 slices hearty whole grain bread, toasted

1 avocado

1. Combine peas, lemon juice, tarragon, ¼ teaspoon salt and pepper in small food processor; pulse until blended but still chunky. Or combine all ingredients in small bowl and mash with fork to desired consistency.

2. Heat oil in small saucepan over medium heat. Add pepitas; cook and stir 1 to 2 minutes or until toasted. Transfer to small bowl; stir in remaining ⅛ teaspoon salt.

3. Spread about 1 tablespoon pea mixture over each slice of bread. If making one serving, place the remaining pea mixture in a jar or container and store in the refrigerator for a day or two.

4. Cut avocado in half lengthwise around pit. If making one serving, wrap the half with the pit in plastic wrap and store in the refrigerator for 1 day. Cut the avocado into slices in the shell; use a spoon to scoop the slices out of the shell. Arrange the slices on the toast; top with toasted pepitas.

Mediterranean Roasted Vegetable Wraps

Makes 4 servings

1 head cauliflower, cut into 1-inch florets

4 tablespoons olive oil, divided

2 teaspoons ras el hanout, 7-spice blend, shawarma blend or za'atar

1 teaspoon salt, divided

1 zucchini, quartered lengthwise and cut into ¼-inch pieces

1 yellow squash, quartered lengthwise and cut into ¼-inch pieces

½ red onion, thinly sliced

¼ cup red pepper sauce (avjar)

4 large thin pita breads or lavash (10 inches)

4 ounces feta cheese, crumbled

1 cup chickpeas

¼ cup diced tomatoes

¼ cup minced fresh parsley

¼ cup diced cucumber (optional)

2 teaspoons vegetable oil

1. Preheat oven to 400°F. Combine cauliflower, 2 tablespoons olive oil, ras el hanout and ½ teaspoon salt in large bowl; toss to coat. Spread on half of sheet pan. Combine zucchini, yellow squash, onion, remaining 2 tablespoons olive oil and ½ teaspoon salt in same bowl; toss to coat. Spread on other side of sheet pan. Roast 25 minutes or until vegetables are browned and tender, stirring once. Remove from oven; cool slightly.

2. Spread 1 tablespoon red pepper sauce on one pita bread. Top with one fourth of vegetables, cheese, chickpeas, tomatoes, parsley and cucumber, if desired. Fold two sides over filling; roll up into burrito shape. Repeat with remaining ingredients.

3. Heat 1 teaspoon vegetable oil in large skillet over medium-high heat. Add two wraps, seam sides down; cook 1 minute or until browned. Turn and cook other side until browned. Repeat with remaining vegetable oil and wraps. Cut in half to serve.

Spinach and Roasted Pepper Panini

Makes 4 servings

1 loaf (12 ounces) focaccia

1½ cups spinach leaves (about 12 leaves)

1 jar (about 7 ounces) roasted red peppers, drained

4 ounces fontina cheese, thinly sliced or sliced provolone-style vegan cheese alternative

¾ cup thinly sliced red onion

Olive oil

1. Cut focaccia in half horizontally. Layer bottom half with spinach, roasted peppers, cheese and onion. Cover with top half of focaccia. Brush outsides of sandwich lightly with oil. Cut sandwich into four pieces.

2. Heat large nonstick skillet over medium heat. Add sandwiches; press down lightly with spatula or weigh down with plate. Cook sandwiches 4 to 5 minutes per side or until cheese melts and bread is golden brown.

Note: Focaccia can be found in the bakery section of most supermarkets. It is often available in different flavors, such as tomato, herb, cheese or onion.

vegetables

Roasted Rainbow Carrots

Makes 4 servings

Carrots

2	**pounds rainbow carrots, peeled and halved if large**
¼	**cup olive oil**
1½	**teaspoons salt**
1	**teaspoon ground cumin**
½	**teaspoon dried thyme**
½	**teaspoon Aleppo pepper or black pepper**

Sauce

2	**tablespoons tahini**
1	**tablespoon lemon juice**
1	**tablespoon maple syrup**
¼	**teaspoon salt**
	Dash ground cumin
2	**tablespoons water**

1. Preheat oven to 400°F. Place carrots on sheet pan; drizzle with oil. Combine 1½ teaspoons salt, 1 teaspoon cumin, thyme and pepper in small bowl. Sprinkle over carrots; roll to coat carrots with oil and seasonings.

2. Roast 20 minutes or until carrots are fork-tender and charred, turning once. Place on serving plate.

3. Meanwhile for sauce, whisk tahini, lemon juice, maple syrup, ¼ teaspoon salt and dash cumin in small bowl. Whisk in water until smooth. Pour over carrots.

Mediterranean-Style Roasted Vegetables

Makes 6 servings

1½ pounds red potatoes, cut into ½-inch chunks

1 tablespoon plus 1½ teaspoons olive oil, divided

1 red bell pepper, cut into ½-inch pieces

1 yellow or orange bell pepper, cut into ½-inch pieces

1 small red onion, cut into ½-inch wedges

2 cloves garlic, minced

½ teaspoon salt

¼ teaspoon black pepper

1 tablespoon balsamic vinegar

¼ cup chopped fresh basil

1. Preheat oven to 425°F. Spray large roasting pan with nonstick cooking spray.

2. Place potatoes in prepared pan. Drizzle with 1 tablespoon oil; toss to coat evenly. Roast 10 minutes.

3. Add bell peppers and onion to pan. Drizzle with remaining 1½ teaspoons oil. Sprinkle with garlic, salt and black pepper; toss to coat evenly.

4. Roast 18 to 20 minutes or until vegetables are browned and tender, stirring once.

5. Transfer vegetables to large serving dish. Drizzle with vinegar; toss to coat evenly. Add basil; toss again. Serve warm or at room temperature.

Sweet Potato Gnocchi

Makes 4 servings (about 40 gnocchi)

1½ pounds sweet potatoes
   (2 or 3 medium)

¼ cup all-purpose flour, plus
   additional for rolling

1 tablespoon lemon juice

1 teaspoon salt

½ teaspoon ground nutmeg

½ teaspoon black pepper

¼ teaspoon sugar

2 to 4 tablespoons olive oil

1 pound spinach, stemmed

1. Preheat oven to 350°F. Bake sweet potatoes 1 hour or until tender.*

2. Cut hot sweet potatoes lengthwise into halves. Scrape pulp from skins into medium bowl. Add ¼ cup flour, lemon juice, salt, nutmeg, pepper and sugar; mix well.

3. Heavily dust cutting board or work surface with flour. Working in batches, scoop portions of dough onto board and roll into ½-inch-thick rope using floured hands. Cut each rope into ¾-inch pieces. Press against tines of fork to make ridges. Freeze gnocchi at least 30 minutes on baking sheet.**

4. Heat 1 tablespoon oil in large nonstick skillet. Add gnocchi in single layer and cook, turning once, until lightly browned and heated through, adding additional oil as needed to prevent sticking. Keep warm.

5. Add remaining 1 tablespoon oil to skillet. Add spinach; cook and stir 30 seconds or until barely wilted. Serve with gnocchi.

Or pierce sweet potatoes several times with fork and place on microwavable plate. Microwave on HIGH 16 to 18 minutes, rotating halfway through cooking time. Let stand 5 minutes.

**Gnocchi may be made ahead to this point and frozen for up to 24 hours. For longer storage, transfer frozen gnocchi to covered freezer container.*

Asparagus with Red Onion, Basil and Almonds

Makes 4 servings

1 tablespoon olive oil

½ cup thinly sliced red onion, separated into rings

¼ cup vegetable broth

1 pound fresh asparagus, trimmed and cut into 1½-inch pieces

2 tablespoons chopped fresh basil

¼ teaspoon salt

¼ teaspoon black pepper

2 tablespoons sliced almonds, toasted*

*To toast almonds, spread in single layer in small heavy skillet. Cook over medium heat 1 to 2 minutes or until lightly browned, stirring frequently. Remove from skillet; cool before using.

1. Heat oil in medium skillet over medium heat. Add onion; cover and cook 5 minutes or until wilted. Uncover; cook 4 to 5 minutes or until onion is tender and golden brown, stirring occasionally.

2. Bring broth to a boil in medium saucepan. Add asparagus; simmer over medium heat 3 minutes. Stir in onion; cook about 2 minutes or until asparagus is crisp-tender and most of liquid has evaporated. Stir in basil, salt and pepper. Sprinkle with almonds.

Cabbage Colcannon

Makes 6 servings

1 pound new red potatoes, halved

1 tablespoon vegetable oil

1 small onion, thinly sliced

½ small head green cabbage, thinly sliced

Salt and black pepper

3 tablespoons butter or vegan plant butter

1. Place potatoes in medium saucepan; add water to cover. Bring to a boil over medium heat; cook 20 minutes or until tender. Drain well.

2. Heat oil in large nonstick skillet over medium-high heat. Add onion; cook and stir 8 minutes or until onion is lightly browned. Add cabbage; cook and stir 5 minutes or until softened.

3. Add potatoes to skillet; cook until heated through. Slightly mash potatoes. Season with salt and pepper. Place ½ tablespoon slice of butter on each portion just before serving.

Portobello Mushrooms Sesame

Makes 4 servings

- **4 large portobello mushrooms**
- **2 tablespoons mirin**
- **2 tablespoons soy sauce**
- **2 cloves garlic, minced**
- **1 teaspoon toasted sesame oil**

1. Prepare grill for direct cooking over medium heat.

2. Remove and discard stems from mushrooms; set caps aside. Whisk mirin, soy sauce, garlic and oil in small bowl until well blended.

3. Brush both sides of mushroom caps with soy sauce mixture. Grill, top sides up, covered, 3 to 4 minutes. Brush tops with soy sauce mixture; turn and grill 2 minutes or until grill marks appear. Turn again and grill 4 to 5 minutes or until tender, basting frequently. Remove mushrooms; cut diagonally into ½-inch-thick slices.

Leeks with Dijon Vinaigrette

Makes 4 servings

4   **leeks**

1   **tablespoon olive oil**

1   **tablespoon red wine vinegar**

¼   **teaspoon Dijon mustard**

⅛   **teaspoon salt**

    Pinch black pepper

1. Trim leek roots; cut leeks lengthwise in half (to about ½ inch from root end), leaving root ends intact. Rinse thoroughly under cold water; drain well. Cut into 1-inch pieces. Arrange in single layer in steamer basket. Steam leeks in large saucepan over boiling water, covered, 10 minutes or until tender when tested with tip of knife. Cool to room temperature or chill.

2. Whisk oil, vinegar, mustard, salt and pepper in small bowl. Spoon over leeks.

Note: Although sometimes sold individually, leeks are usually displayed in bunches of 3 or 4. The smaller the leek, the more tender it will be. Leeks more than 1½ inches in diameter can be tough and woody. Choose ones with firm bright green stalks and white blemish-free bases. Avoid leeks with split or oversized bases.

Creamy Parmesan Spinach

Makes 6 servings

- 2 tablespoons butter, divided
- 1 cup finely chopped yellow onion
- 2 packages (9 ounces each) fresh spinach, divided
- 3 ounces cream cheese, cut into pieces
- ½ teaspoon garlic powder
- ¼ teaspoon ground nutmeg
- ¼ teaspoon black pepper
- ⅛ teaspoon salt
- 2 tablespoons grated Parmesan, pecorino or Monterey Jack cheese

1. Melt 1 tablespoon butter in large skillet over medium-high heat. Add onion; cook and stir 4 minutes or until translucent.

2. Add 1 package of spinach; cook and stir 2 minutes or just until wilted. Transfer spinach mixture to medium bowl. Repeat with remaining 1 tablespoon butter and spinach.

3. Return reserved spinach to skillet. Add cream cheese, garlic powder, nutmeg, pepper and salt; cook and stir until cream cheese has completely melted.

4. Sprinkle with cheese just before serving.

Variation: For a thinner consistency, add 2 to 3 tablespoons milk before adding the Parmesan cheese.

Couscous and Spinach Stuffed Peppers

Makes 4 servings

¾ cup uncooked couscous

1 tablespoon canola oil

½ cup finely chopped onion

3 cups (4 ounces) fresh spinach, chopped *or* 4 ounces frozen spinach, chopped

1 teaspoon dried oregano

½ teaspoon salt

2¼ cups water, divided

4 medium bell peppers, any color

Sauce

½ cup drained jarred roasted peppers

½ cup tomato sauce

½ teaspoon ground red pepper (optional)

Salt and black pepper

1. Heat large nonstick skillet over medium-high heat. Add couscous; lightly roast about 5 minutes, stirring occasionally. Transfer to plate; set aside.

2. Heat oil in same skillet over medium-high heat. Add onion; cook and stir 2 to 3 minutes or until onion is translucent. Add spinach, oregano and salt; cook and stir 1 to 2 minutes or until spinach is wilted. Add 2 cups water; bring to a boil. Stir in couscous; remove from heat. Cover and let stand 5 to 7 minutes or until water is absorbed.

3. Cut off ½ inch from tops of bell peppers and remove seeds and membranes. Fill peppers with couscous mixture; cover with tops. Place peppers in deep skillet or saucepan that holds peppers upright. Add remaining ¼ cup water to skillet; bring to a boil over medium-high heat. Cover tightly with lid; cook 8 to 9 minutes or until peppers are slightly softened. Remove peppers to serving dish.

4. Meanwhile for sauce, place roasted peppers, tomato sauce and ground red pepper, if desired, in food processor. Cover; process until smooth. Transfer to small saucepan; cook and stir over medium heat until heated through. Season with salt and black pepper. Serve with stuffed peppers.

Vegetable Tart

Makes 16 servings

1 teaspoon active dry yeast

⅓ cup warm water (115°F)

1 egg, beaten

3 tablespoons sour cream

1¼ cups all-purpose flour

¼ cup whole wheat flour

¾ teaspoon salt, divided

1 small sweet potato, peeled and cut crosswise into ¼-inch slices

2 tablespoons olive oil, divided

1 cup sliced mushrooms

½ cup thinly sliced leeks

1 medium zucchini, sliced

1 parsnip, sliced

1 medium red bell pepper, cut into 1-inch pieces

8 to 10 cloves garlic, minced

1 teaspoon dried basil

½ teaspoon dried rosemary

Black pepper)

2 to 4 tablespoons grated Parmesan cheese

1 egg white, beaten

1. Preheat oven to 400°F. Sprinkle yeast over warm water in medium bowl; stir until yeast is dissolved. Let stand 5 minutes or until mixture is bubbly. Add egg and sour cream; mix until smooth. Add flours and ¼ teaspoon salt; stir to form soft dough. Turn out onto lightly floured surface; knead 1 to 2 minutes or until smooth. Shape dough into a ball; place in large lightly greased bowl. Turn dough over to grease top. Cover bowl with towel; let rest in warm place 20 minutes.

2. Spray large rimmed baking sheet with nonstick cooking spray. Place sweet potato slices in single layer on prepared baking sheet; drizzle with 1 tablespoon oil and toss to coat. Bake 15 to 20 minutes or until potatoes are tender, turning once.

3. Heat remaining 1 tablespoon oil in large skillet over medium heat. Add mushrooms, leeks, zucchini, parsnip, bell pepper, garlic, basil and rosemary; cook and stir 8 to 10 minutes or until vegetables are tender. Season with remaining ½ teaspoon salt and black pepper.

4. Roll out dough into 14-inch round on lightly floured surface; place on baking sheet or large pizza pan. Arrange sweet potato slices evenly over crust, leaving 2½-inch border. Spoon vegetable mixture evenly over potatoes; sprinkle with cheese. Fold edge of dough over edge of vegetable mixture, pleating dough as necessary, to fit. Brush edge of dough with egg white.

5. Bake 25 minutes or until golden brown. Cut into wedges; serve warm.

Roasted Cinnamon Sweet Potatoes with Onions

Makes 6 servings

2 **pounds sweet potatoes, peeled**

1 **sweet onion, cut into eighths**

2 **cloves garlic, chopped**

¼ **cup olive oil**

2 **tablespoons orange juice**

½ **teaspoon ground cinnamon**

Salt and black pepper

1. Preheat oven to 400°F. Cut potatoes in half lengthwise, then into 1-inch-thick slices.

2. Place potatoes, onion and garlic in 12×8-inch baking dish. Drizzle with oil; toss to coat. Sprinkle with orange juice, cinnamon, salt and pepper; toss until well coated.

3. Cover with foil; bake 35 to 40 minutes or until potatoes are tender.

Moroccan Chickpeas

Makes 6 servings

1 cup chopped onion

¼ cup vegetable broth

2 cloves garlic, crushed

2 cans (about 15 ounces each) chickpeas, rinsed and drained

1 can (28 ounces) diced tomatoes

½ cup sliced red bell pepper

½ cup sliced yellow bell pepper

½ cup sliced green bell pepper

2 tablespoons oil-cured olives, pitted and chopped

1 teaspoon ground cumin

1 teaspoon ground ginger

1 teaspoon ground turmeric

¼ teaspoon salt

1 bay leaf

2 tablespoons lemon juice

1. Combine onion, broth and garlic in large nonstick skillet. Cook and stir over medium heat 3 minutes or until onion softens.

2. Add chickpeas, tomatoes, bell peppers, olives, cumin, ginger, turmeric, salt and bay leaf. Stir well. Simmer 5 minutes or until bell peppers are tender. Remove and discard bay leaf. Stir in lemon juice; adjust seasonings.

snacks

Onion and White Bean Spread

Makes 1¼ cups spread

1 can (about 15 ounces) cannellini or Great Northern beans, rinsed and drained

¼ cup chopped green onions

¼ cup grated Parmesan cheese

¼ cup olive oil, plus additional for serving

1 tablespoon fresh rosemary, chopped

2 cloves garlic, minced

French bread slices

1. Combine beans, green onions, cheese, ¼ cup oil, rosemary and garlic in food processor; process 30 to 40 seconds or until almost smooth.

2. Spoon bean mixture into serving bowl. Drizzle with additional oil just before serving. Serve with bread.

Tip: For a more rustic-looking spread, place all ingredients in a medium bowl and mash them with a potato masher.

Margherita Pizza with Quinoa Crust

Makes 4 servings

1 cup uncooked quinoa

⅓ cup water, plus additional for soaking

1 teaspoon baking powder

¾ teaspoon salt

1 tablespoon olive oil, plus drizzle for serving

½ cup marinara sauce

1 ball (8 ounces) fresh mozzarella cheese, cut into ¼-inch-thick slices

Fresh basil leaves, flaky sea salt and freshly ground black pepper (optional)

1. Place quinoa in medium bowl; cover with 1 inch of water. Cover bowl; let soak 8 hours or overnight at room temperature. Rinse well and drain.

2. Combine soaked quinoa, ⅓ cup water, baking powder and salt in food processor. Process 2 minutes or until completely smooth, stopping to scrape side of bowl as needed.

3. Preheat oven to 450°F. Line bottom of 10-inch springform pan with foil. Brush with 1 tablespoon oil. Attach sides of pan. Pour quinoa mixture into pan, using spatula to spread over bottom. Bake 10 to 12 minutes or until quinoa is golden on sides and bottom.

4. Remove pan from oven. Remove side of pan. Spread marinara sauce evenly over crust. Top with cheese. Bake 10 minutes or until cheese is melted and bottom of crust is golden brown.

5. Slide pizza onto large cutting board. Top with basil and additional oil. Sprinkle with sea salt and pepper, if desired. Slice and serve immediately.

Quick and Easy Stuffed Mushrooms

Makes 16 mushrooms

  1 slice whole wheat bread
 16 large mushrooms
 ½ cup sliced celery
 ½ cup sliced onion
  1 clove garlic
  1 tablespoon olive oil
  1 teaspoon soy sauce
 ½ teaspoon dried marjoram
 ⅛ teaspoon ground red pepper
    Salt and black pepper
    Paprika

1. Tear bread into pieces; place in food processor. Process 30 seconds or until crumbs are formed. Transfer to medium bowl.

2. Remove stems from mushrooms; reserve caps. Place mushroom stems, celery, onion and garlic in food processor; process using on/off pulses until vegetables are finely chopped.

3. Heat oil in large skillet over medium heat. Add vegetable mixture; cook and stir 5 minutes or until onion is tender. Add to bread crumbs. Stir in soy sauce, marjoram and red pepper. Season with salt and black pepper.

4. Fill mushroom caps evenly with mixture, pressing down firmly. Place about ½ inch apart in shallow baking pan. Spray tops with nonstick cooking spray. Sprinkle with paprika.

5. Preheat oven to 350°F. Bake 15 minutes or until heated through.

Note: Mushrooms can be stuffed up to 24 hours ahead. Refrigerate filled mushroom caps, covered, until ready to serve. Bake in preheated 300°F oven 20 minutes or until heated through.

Classic Guacamole

Makes about 2 cups

- **4** tablespoons finely chopped white onion, divided
- **1** to 2 serrano or jalapeño peppers, seeded and finely chopped
- **1½** tablespoons coarsely chopped fresh cilantro, divided
- **¼** teaspoon chopped garlic (optional)
- **2** large ripe avocados
- **1** medium tomato, peeled and chopped
- **1** to 2 teaspoons fresh lime juice
- **¼** teaspoon salt

  Tortilla chips and/or cut-up fresh vegetables for dipping

1. Combine 2 tablespoons onion, serrano pepper, 1 tablespoon cilantro and garlic, if desired, in large mortar. Grind with pestle until almost smooth. (Mixture can be processed in food processor, if necessary, but it may become more watery than desired.)

2. Cut avocados into halves; remove and discard pits. Scoop out pulp; place in large bowl. Add pepper mixture; mash roughly, leaving avocado slightly chunky.

3. Add tomato, lime juice, salt, remaining 2 tablespoons onion and ½ tablespoon cilantro to avocado mixture; mix well. Serve immediately with tortilla chips or cover and refrigerate up to 4 hours.

Tuscan White Bean Crostini

Makes 18 crostini

2 cans (about 15 ounces each) cannellini or Great Northern beans, rinsed and drained

½ large red bell pepper, finely chopped *or* ⅓ cup finely chopped roasted red bell pepper

⅓ cup finely chopped onion

⅓ cup red wine vinegar

3 tablespoons chopped fresh parsley

1 tablespoon olive oil

2 cloves garlic, minced

½ teaspoon dried oregano

¼ teaspoon black pepper

18 slices French bread, about ¼ inch thick

1. Combine beans, bell pepper and onion in large bowl.

2. Whisk vinegar, parsley, oil, garlic, oregano and black pepper in small bowl. Pour over bean mixture; toss to coat. Cover and refrigerate 2 hours or overnight.

3. Preheat broiler. Arrange bread slices in single layer on large baking sheet or broiler pan. Broil 6 to 8 inches from heat 30 to 45 seconds or until lightly toasted. Cool completely.

4. Top each toasted bread slice with bean mixture.

Cheddar Crackers

Makes 24 crackers

1½ cups brown rice flour

1 teaspoon garlic powder

1 teaspoon Italian seasoning

½ teaspoon salt

6 tablespoons (¾ stick) cold butter, cut into ½-inch cubes

½ cup (2 ounces) finely grated sharp Cheddar cheese

½ cup cold water

1. Combine brown rice flour, garlic powder, Italian seasoning and salt in food processor or blender; process until well blended. Add butter and cheese; pulse until coarse crumbs form. Add water; process until dough forms.

2. Divide dough into two pieces; wrap in plastic wrap and refrigerate 20 minutes.

3. Preheat oven to 350°F. Line baking sheets with parchment paper.

4. Place each dough half between two pieces of parchment paper; roll out to ¹⁄₁₆-inch thickness. Refrigerate 5 minutes.

5. Cut dough into 2½-inch squares; place on prepared baking sheets.

6. Bake 15 minutes or until golden and crisp, rotating baking sheets after 10 minutes. Cool on baking sheets 10 minutes. Remove to wire racks; cool completely.

Buffalo Wedges

Makes 4 servings

3 pounds unpeeled Yukon Gold potatoes

3 tablespoons hot pepper sauce

2 tablespoons butter or vegan plant butter, melted

2 teaspoons smoked or sweet paprika

½ teaspoon salt

Blue cheese dressing (regular or vegan)

1. Preheat oven to 400°F. Spray baking sheet with nonstick cooking spray. Cut each potato into 4 to 6 wedges, depending on size of potato.

2. Combine hot pepper sauce, butter, paprika and salt in large bowl. Add potato wedges; toss to coat well. Place wedges in single layer on prepared baking sheet.

3. Bake 20 minutes. Turn potatoes; bake 20 minutes or until light golden brown and crisp. Serve with blue cheese dressing.

Roasted Sweet Potato and Hoisin Lettuce Wraps

Makes 4 servings

1 to 2 large sweet potatoes (about 12 ounces), cut into ½-inch cubes

1 large onion, cut into 8 wedges

2 tablespoons vegetable oil, divided

Salt and black pepper

¼ cup water

¼ cup creamy peanut butter

3 tablespoons hoisin sauce

2 tablespoons lime juice

3 cloves garlic, minced

1 tablespoon ketchup

2 teaspoons grated fresh ginger

⅛ teaspoon red pepper flakes

12 large Bibb lettuce leaves, rinsed and patted dry

2 cups shredded cabbage or packaged coleslaw

½ cup julienned or shredded carrots

½ cup dry-roasted peanuts

1. Preheat oven to 425°F. Line baking sheet with foil. Place potatoes and onion on baking sheet. Drizzle with 1 tablespoon oil and season with salt and pepper; toss to coat. Roast 20 minutes or until edges of onion begin to brown and potatoes are tender, stirring once halfway through cooking time.

2. Meanwhile for sauce, combine water, peanut butter, hoisin, lime juice, garlic, remaining 1 tablespoon oil, ketchup, ginger and red pepper flakes in small bowl; whisk until well blended.

3. To serve, top each lettuce leaf with cabbage, sweet potato mixture and carrots. Drizzle with 1 tablespoon sauce and sprinkle with peanuts. Fold bottom over filling, then fold two sides up to form bundles.

Black Bean Salsa

Makes 6 servings

1 can (about 15 ounces) black
   beans, rinsed and drained

1 cup fresh or thawed frozen
   corn

1 tomato, chopped

¼ cup chopped green onions

2 tablespoons chopped fresh
   cilantro

2 tablespoons lemon juice

1 tablespoon vegetable oil

1 teaspoon chili powder

¼ teaspoon salt

6 corn tortillas

   Lime wedges (optional)

1. Combine beans, corn, tomato, green onions, cilantro, lemon juice, oil, chili powder and salt in medium bowl; mix well.

2. Preheat oven to 400°F. Cut each tortilla into 8 wedges; place on ungreased baking sheet. Bake 6 to 8 minutes or until edges begin to brown; cool slightly. Serve tortilla wedges with salsa. Garnish with lime wedges.

Creamy Maple Berries

Makes 4 servings

½ cup sour cream or plain yogurt (regular or vegan)

2 tablespoons maple syrup

2 cups halved fresh strawberries

1 cup fresh blueberries

1. Combine sour cream and maple syrup in small bowl.

2. Combine strawberries and blueberries in medium bowl; toss gently. Spoon berries into four bowls; top with sour cream mixture.

metric conversion chart

VOLUME MEASUREMENTS (dry)

⅛ teaspoon = 0.5 mL
¼ teaspoon = 1 mL
½ teaspoon = 2 mL
¾ teaspoon = 4 mL
1 teaspoon = 5 mL
1 tablespoon = 15 mL
2 tablespoons = 30 mL
¼ cup = 60 mL
⅓ cup = 75 mL
½ cup = 125 mL
⅔ cup = 150 mL
¾ cup = 175 mL
1 cup = 250 mL
2 cups = 1 pint = 500 mL
3 cups = 750 mL
4 cups = 1 quart = 1 L

VOLUME MEASUREMENTS (fluid)

1 fluid ounce (2 tablespoons) = 30 mL
4 fluid ounces (½ cup) = 125 mL
8 fluid ounces (1 cup) = 250 mL
12 fluid ounces (1½ cups) = 375 mL
16 fluid ounces (2 cups) = 500 mL

WEIGHTS (mass)

½ ounce = 15 g
1 ounce = 30 g
3 ounces = 90 g
4 ounces = 120 g
8 ounces = 225 g
10 ounces = 285 g
12 ounces = 360 g
16 ounces = 1 pound = 450 g

DIMENSIONS

1/16 inch = 2 mm
⅛ inch = 3 mm
¼ inch = 6 mm
½ inch = 1.5 cm
¾ inch = 2 cm
1 inch = 2.5 cm

OVEN TEMPERATURES

250°F = 120°C
275°F = 140°C
300°F = 150°C
325°F = 160°C
350°F = 180°C
375°F = 190°C
400°F = 200°C
425°F = 220°C
450°F = 230°C

BAKING PAN SIZES

Utensil	Size in Inches/Quarts	Metric Volume	Size in Centimeters
Baking or Cake Pan (square or rectangular)	8×8×2	2 L	20×20×5
	9×9×2	2.5 L	23×23×5
	12×8×2	3 L	30×20×5
	13×9×2	3.5 L	33×23×5
Loaf Pan	8×4×3	1.5 L	20×10×7
	9×5×3	2 L	23×13×7
Round Layer Cake Pan	8×1½	1.2 L	20×4
	9×1½	1.5 L	23×4
Pie Plate	8×1¼	750 mL	20×3
	9×1¼	1 L	23×3
Baking Dish or Casserole	1 quart	1 L	—
	1½ quart	1.5 L	—
	2 quart	2 L	—